Previously by Jason Moss

Smell & Bogey and the Magic Carpet

and the Missing Slippers

Jason Moss

Illustrated by Steven Hier

Visit Smell & Bogey at:
www.smellandbogey.com

Published in 2015 by New Generation Publishing

Text © Jason Moss 2015
Illustrations © Steven Hier 2015

First Edition

The author and illustrator asserts the moral right under
the Copyright, Designs and Patents Act 1988 to be
Identified as the author and illustrator of this work.

All rights reserved. No part of this publication may be
Reproduced, stored in a retrieval system, or transmitted, in
Any form or by any means without the prior written consent
of the author, nor be otherwise circulated in any form of
binding or cover other than that in which it is published and
without a similar condition being imposed on the subsequent
purchaser.

For Bab

Preface

The dust had settled and everything was back in its rightful place. The Magic Carpet was peaceful again. Smell and Bogey's little green Monopoly house stood proud, hugged by the tall woolly threads of magical carpet that surrounded it. A neatly trimmed lawn of carpet led to a solitary white painted gate: no fencing, just the gate remained, awkward but steadfast. Life had got back to its normal humdrum of routines and day-to-day chores, which bored the hover-pants off Smell but delighted Bogey. Order, calm and tranquillity - just the way Bogey liked it! Not the perfect setting for an exciting adventure I hear you cry – but that was all about to change at this year's annual Carpet Slipper Race!

Chapter One

The Carpet Slipper Race

'Well welcome everybody to the forty-ninth annual Carpet Slipper Race and what promises to be the most exciting racing in years!' announced Herron over the tannoy in the commentary box. His craggy voice echoed for miles around the Magic Carpet. A lively crowd had gathered in the arena, all cheering and screaming with excitement. Spirits were high. Anticipation filled the air.

'Yes that's right Herron... *HICCUP!*' announced Finch. 'Reining champions Whiff and Whatnot are looking better than ever before with a whole year of gruelling training deep in the Twisted Forest under their belts. They're in great... *HICCUP...* shape, with all eyes firmly on the favourites yet again. But can they make it five years in a row?' The dim-witted Fleas, one short and fat, the other tall and skinny, both picked their noses as they watched the contenders gather in the arena.

Whiff and Whatnot waved regally at the crowd as they paraded into the arena. Whiff resembled a tall and wobbly gust of wind with enormously long hairs dangling from his nose. He looked terribly dim... and *he* was the clever one! Whatnot on the other hand was almost indescribable - a splodgey lump of gooey, bluey, browny gunk, covered in bits and bobs picked up from the carpet who would change shape every time he moved. He was the less intelligent of the pair but you wouldn't want to mess with him - he could explode into violent fits of rage at any given moment.

Finch took a swig from his big glass of water as another hiccup threatened to erupt. He grinned at Herron and then... *HICCUP!*

Heron's big belly bulged over the desk in the commentary box, his blood red eyes wide open with excitement. Finch picked his nose again and nibbled on the contents sitting on his finger.

'Will you stop nibbling and concentrate?!' shouted Heron.

The Magic Carpet was now packed out with thousands of carpet dwellers. All shapes and sizes congregated around a playing field. Everyone was dressed up in their favourite outfits. Colourful bunting decorated the tall carpet threads and all sorts of stalls lined the arena selling the strangest of snacks:
roasted toenail clippings, snotty floss on sticks, juicy blackheads and even balls of bumf, which was anything you could find that was barely edible and dunked in treacle.

'Well there's certainly some stiff competition this year, Finch. The race is wide open with some amazing new talent on the scene ready to challenge the champions.' Herron pointed at the parade of contenders as they entered the showground, each of them wearing brightly coloured jerseys and multi-coloured hats. Some were waving banners and flags to the crowd. A roar of support from the spectators lifted the atmosphere.

'You're not wrong Herron... *HICCUP*! For the first time in its forty-nine year history, we have dust mites racing in the Carpet Slipper Race!' A few people in the crowd booed and jeered, followed by laughter at the sight of Team Dust Mite entering the arena.

'Gnarl and Barkley are both from south of the Magic Carpet and boast the fastest slippers around... *HICCUP!* Their only weakness will be arguing during the race. Once they start bickering they can kiss goodbye to that trophy.'

'Yes the Carpet Slipper Trophy remains the most sort after prize in the Magic Carpet!' announced Herron with pride. 'Only the greatest athletes manage to hold aloft this prestigious award and gain entry into Farty Bumflump's Hall of Fame!' He looked over at a golden pair of slippers strapped to a golden stand, gleaming in the sunlight for all to see. Strapped to the stand was a wooden shield and etched onto the shield read the words: *Farty Bumflump's Golden Slippers 1859.*

In the centre of the huge arena was a spiralling pathway leading off into the depths of the Magic Carpet. At the centre stood a flagpole with a woolly flag waving in the morning breeze. On the flag was sewn a coat of arms bearing the letters M.C. and underneath was a wooden podium decorated with colourful bunting flapping in the wind.

'*HICCUP!* And look! Here's another two new contenders to this year's race. Making his debut and supported by his father Fangs, it's little Legs!' A roar of cheering echoed around the carpet as sixteen pairs of legs and sixteen pairs of eyes come into view.

'Yes Finch! A very popular team in this year's event and little Legs is another new edition to the spider family. He's proven very fast in this year's trials too, but doubts over his stamina still remain.'

'I'm told he's been a strain on the family budget too, getting through four pairs of slippers every practice!' announced Finch looking closer at the contenders who were now lined up in the centre of the track, limbering up like fidgeting maggots.

'Wait! There's one team missing from this afternoon's parade… No showing for Bogey and Smell this year? *HICCUP!*' A gasp rumbled from the crowd.

Herron looked up and down the line of at least a hundred contenders. He looked puzzled.

'Surely Bogey wouldn't miss the Carpet Slipper Race? He may have been humiliated last year by coming last, but then again he always comes last and he has said on record that this year is going to be his year.' said Heron.

'He said that last year! replied Finch, 'Anyway, there's nothing in the rules that says you have to turn up for the opening parade, but he races tomorrow so I hope he's getting in some extra practice… *HICCUP!*'

The Carpet Slipper Race was the biggest event of the year. Thousands would come from miles around to watch, bet and to soak up the atmosphere. People would dress up in their best outfits, mingle and socialise, whilst watching the competitors race through courses mapped out in the Magic Carpet. I say race, but it was more like fast walking in your slippers. Can you really imagine someone like Bogey moving fast for anything other than food?!

Herron tapped the microphone. A high-pitched whistle echoed around the arena deafening the spectators. 'Err, sorry bout that,' said Herron. 'Now this year's sponsor for the Carpet Slipper Race is none other than Zodiac Racing who have kindly donated all of the footwear for the competitors, so a big thank you to Zodiac…'

'Yes, but which slipper will prove to be the fastest, Zodiac Flash or Zodiac White Stripe? *HICCUP!*' said Finch.

'Well it looks like we're about to find out, Finch. The Mayor is at the microphone and ready to give his annual address…'

A bald, short and fat character wobbled onto the podium in the centre of the arena, accompanied by his spindly and very nervous looking wife. He wore enormous round spectacles and had a massive moustache that curled up at the ends. He wore a suit on his top half and summer shorts on his bottom half, revealing his little hairy legs. Shiny black polished shoes gleamed in the morning light and socks fastened by elasticated garters were pulled up to his knobbly knees. Around his neck he wore his mayoral golden chain. What a funny sight indeed! The mayor waved to the cheering and jeering crowd, loving every minute of his fame.

His wife really didn't look comfortable at all. She was pale and thin. In fact she was so thin that if she turned sideways she'd literally disappear. She wobbled in her red high heels, clutching her belly with nerves. She'd only been off the toilet a few minutes and didn't quite know if she could survive all the formalities. Then the Mayor spoke into the microphone…

'Lemons and Mentle-jen… *Argh hum*! Firstly may I japolise most sincerely for my awful munchies that I brung to you on this, the most hideous of caucations!'

The crowd looked puzzled as the mayor addressed the arena. His wife quickly handed him a handkerchief, which he blew into, creating an enormous foghorn sound that went whizzing into the microphone. The entire crowd dropped to the floor in pain and agony, deafened from the nosey outburst. Sorry, *noisy* outburst.

'Japa-logeys, my sincere japa-logeys! My wife and I have come down with the flapjacks, suffering in synchronisation... *Argh-hum*! I mean... We have been raising the agents, in conjunction with, or contention of, any part, to be hereby referred to as the undersigned. I mean, have been... Under the weather! We've been surfing with a bout of *Word Flu*... Err, my doctor's crazy paving assures me it's not serious or contagious, exchangeable or convertible and any assignable notions or motions on our part are due to our jumbles getting worded up in the process.'

The crowd looked bewildered and confused as the mayor proudly twiddled with his enormous moustache, glancing around the arena.

'It's indeed an honour and a fishcake to be flapping with so many scrawny looking toenails today... My wife and I are miserable to be nibbling on your most hideous of rabbit droppings!'

'Blow your nose my dear, you're getting all bunged up again,' whispered Mrs Mayor as she handed him a clean hanky.

'Thank you my dreary strife,' whispered the mayor. He cleared his throat and went to speak again.

'It's so woeful to see so many mad badgers – athletes', he corrected himself, 'all trying so hard to jumble about with their brollies on this monumental panda.'

'GET OFF!' shouted one of the dust mites in the crowd.

'Err, I wish you all the biggest pile of dung beetles in your endeavours to be rancid and may the biggest lowlife creep win the honour of all those who sail in your grandmother's undergarments!'

'BOO!' The crowd started to get restless and disgruntled as the mayor's speech became more and more garbled. One multi-legged caterpillar threw several slippers onto the podium, narrowly missing the mayor. Then a dust mite threw a pineapple, then came a flying tomato. It whizzed through the air and landed on Mrs Mayor's face. She gasped with the shock, accidentally sucking up the rotten tomato and swallowing it whole. Suddenly a creamy cake landed on Mr Mayor's knobbly knee and before you knew it, hundreds of carpet folk were hurling allsorts of edible objects at the distinguished couple.

'Lemons and Mentle-jen, settle down per…lease!'

SPLAT! went a giant tomato right in Mr Mayor's face.

'Err, we better get off my dear,' he whispered to his wife, who was now bright orange with tomato stains.

'I knew I shouldn't have worn me bestest frock!' she thought as she crept off the podium trying to balance herself in her high-heels.

'I now declare the forty-ninth Carpet Slipper Race open. Let the games begin!' shouted the mayor.

A roar of cheering erupted from the crowd and echoed into the Magic Carpet. The contenders in the arena set off on their opening parade, proudly waving at the crowds whilst the Ant Army band played a rousing marching theme.

'Smelly, help me quick! Come quickly!' echoed Bogey's troubled voice from inside the little green Monopoly house. His voice went whizzing into the bedroom where Smell sat on his bed looking terribly miserable and clutching a snotty hanky. Smell looked up slowly, his eyes droopy and his nose shining a bright red like a ripened cherry.

'Smelly! Quickly!' came Bogey's voice again. Suddenly a crash came from the kitchen and then a smash as the whole house shuddered and wobbled from side to side…

Smell looked very pale and very transparent. His usual glow was dimmed, bags were drooping under his eyes and despite being the smell of smelly feet even his gentle pong had faded. He slowly forced himself up off his bed and plodded carefully down the stairs in his favourite underpants. He walked into a dusty kitchen feeling very sorry for himself.

'Smogey?!' yelled Smell. 'Smogey?!' he yelled again, slightly louder this time.

'Smelly, quick get me down from here! I'm stuck and I can't move at all!' replied Bogey's voice. Smell could not see a thing with all the dust that had engulfed the kitchen.

'Where are you?' he yelled again, holding onto the kitchen door not daring to enter.

'I'm up here! Can't you see me legs?' Smell looked up slowly to where the voice appeared to be coming from and suddenly caught a glimpse of two green stumpy legs dangling from the ceiling.

'Flop in the mouldy old carcass are you fiddling up there?' Smell waved his hands to try and clear a way through the dust. As he walked into the kitchen, he stumped his toe on the kitchen dresser. 'Owe!' he yelled.

'I thought I'd try on your hover pants for size but I couldn't control them and ended up bouncing up and down until my head got stuck in the ceiling,' moaned Bogey as he wriggled to try and break free. As the dust started to clear, Smell could see the full extent of the damage. Bogey's head was completely jammed through a hole in the kitchen ceiling, his big bulging belly wobbling like jelly and a pair of white Y-front-underpants stretching to bursting point around his waist. Below, two stumpy green legs dangled.

'Bot a tripe you are Smogey. How is I sausage wobble to bananas you down from there?' wibbled Smell.

'Blimey Smelly, you're word flu is getting worst. You're wibbling all over the place. Have you taken that medicine I made for you yet?' Bogey was very domestic, he didn't like adventure and unlike Smell, who craved excitement; the only thing Bogey craved was eating and sleeping.

'Snow grapes me pancakes, the taste is like left over chewy earwax!' Smell wibbled again. Word flu plays havoc with your sentences. The symptoms are just like normal flu, with all the usual snot and dribble, followed by a couple of days of getting your birds jumbled up. Sorry... words jumbled up!

'Well you better take that medicine quick, cause I can't understand a word you're saying and I can't hang around here all day! Look at the time! I'm supposed to be at the opening ceremony!' Bogey looked over to his new pair of shiny slippers neatly tucked up against the kitchen wall by the fireplace. A brand new pair of *Zodiac - White Stripe* waited patiently, still in their protective packaging. A white stripy line ran down the side of a pair of red and green tartan slippers. On the back were the words: *Bogey 13.*

Smell looked around the kitchen for a suitable utensil to help prise Bogey out from his hole. Have you ever picked a bogey from it's whole before? Precise prodding is required, especially when you're Bogey' size. His snotty green complexion had faded a little but he was still very very large.

'Ah! This'll do it!' shouted Smell, grabbing hold of the kitchen broom.

'No! You can't prod me with that thing! I'll fall!' yelled Bogey as a huge crack appeared in the ceiling.

'Well wizzell flip me biggin... No, wait... Well what do you expect me to do? You've got to be prised out or you'll miss the Carpet Slipper Race!' Smell inched nearer to Bogey's big green bottom with the pointy end of the broomstick.

'Put something below me to catch me when I fall then. Otherwise I'll flatten the kitchen table!' screamed Bogey.

Smell put down the broom and set about designing the softest surface for Bogey to land on. Tea towels, cushions, blankets and even Bogey's favourite beanbag were all heaped together in the centre of the kitchen to make a soft landing.

'There. Will that do?' asked Smell, as he grabbed hold of the broom again, eager to give Bogey a good prodding. All the excitement was doing his word flu the power of good.

'NO!' yelled Bogey again. 'I'm not in line with the cushions!' Suddenly another crack appeared in the ceiling, then another started to tear its way through the plaster meeting the other crack in the centre where Bogey was dangling. From outside their house, a deep rumbling rattled the front door, shaking it on its hinges. Then the whole house shuddered. Bogey tried to grab onto something but there was nothing to grab. *'KNOCK KNOCK KNOCK!'* boomed the front door, followed by a very familiar voice.

'Smell! Bogey! Let me in quick! It's… too… windy out here… HELP!' A strong gust of wind suddenly buffeted the house from side to side. Smell quickly leapt to the rescue, running toward the door. He could just see through the kitchen window that a gale was blowing outside, churning up dust and debris in the front garden, with Fluff caught in the middle of it! Smell could see her beautiful brown eyes wide open in fear, she was holding onto the doorknocker of the little green house with all the strength she had, but her legs were waving in the air as she buffeted in the wind. Being a lovely ball of fluff had its disadvantages, especially in high winds.

'Boges, it's Fluff!' yelled Smell as he unlatched the door in haste.

'NO DON'T!' shrieked Bogey as the kitchen door blew wide open, almost coming off its hinges. The entire door slammed against the kitchen wall with an almighty bang. In rushed an enormous gust of wind blowing Fluff into Smell and Smell into Bogey's pile of cushions and blankets, they suddenly caught the wind and took to the air. Whirling around the kitchen like a Merry-go-round. All this commotion is too much for the already weakened ceiling and with an almighty creak, then a very loud crack… Bogey fell from his hole bringing half the ceiling down with him. He crashed onto the kitchen floor with a noisy THUD! The floorboards snapped and creaked and then, with the enormous strain, the floorboards gave way and poor old Bogey fell straight through into the room below…

AAAGGGHHHH! CRASH!

Chapter Two

Missing Slippers

'Help...' whimpered Bogey, dazed and bewildered sitting in the dark place.

'Bogey, are you alright?' yelled Fluff, looking concerned as she peered through the gaping hole in the kitchen floor. Smell joined her at the edge and gawped in.

'Blimey! Those floorboards were weak. Or you're getting fatter!' he yelled down at Bogey. 'I didn't know we had a basement?'

'Ow! I landed on me essentials!' called out Bogey, looking up at his two friends.

'What are your essentials?' cried Fluff concerned.

'Me secret stash of biscuits! I always carry a few in me pockets and now they're all in bits!' Fluff looked at Smell and raised an eyebrow.

'Are *you* alright?' called Smell sarcastically.

'Yes, I'm alright, but...'

'What?' shouted Fluff.

'Bogey!' yelled Smell. There was silence below.

Fluff and Smell both yelled as loudly as they could.

'BOGEY!' they screamed in panic.

'Yeah! What?' came Bogey's voice again. Smell and Fluff breathed a sigh of relief. Just then the front door buffeted against the kitchen wall. The wind was still blowing fiercely outside. Smell went to close it and stared for a moment out into the surrounding forest, thinking he'd seen movement in the trees. But everything was moving - there was a ferocious gale blowing and all the carpet threads were waving and flapping in the storm.

'Fluff, Smell, take a look at what's down here!' cried Bogey in amazement.

'What is it?' called Fluff.

'Get a torch, quick!' Smell found an old rusty torch and peered down the hole, shining the pale beam of light towards Bogey who was now standing up and gazing in wonder at the sight before his eyes.

Down in the basement they never new they had, shelves lined every wall from floor to ceiling. Neatly placed on each shelf were hundreds and hundreds of old carpet slippers. Bogey dribbled with excitement.

'Look at this lot!' he yelled. 'Throw me that torch quick!' Catching the torch, Bogey hurried to shine the light along the wall of slippers: there was every possible design, shape and size you could imagine, all perfectly preserved and neatly displayed. It was like a museum for slippers. Some of them were very old and covered in dust, one pair was made of wood (they were more like clogs than slippers) and another pair had the name Geraldine Cramp with the number 56 written on the back.

'Guys, these are other peoples' slippers from years gone by. There's a pair here dating from the early nineteen hundreds!' said Bogey, his voice echoing in the cold, gloomy basement.

As Bogey shone his torch along the wall of slippers, he realised the shelves went on far past the beam of his light. He shone the torch up and again more shelves and again more and more slippers…

'This is weird!' thought Bogey. He'd started to feel a little bit uncomfortable about the whole thing. 'Who would collect all these slippers? And why?' Something didn't feel right and Bogey was standing in the middle of it.

Just then something caught Bogey's eye... A flash of gold dazzled him for a second. He inched slowly over to another pair of very old-fashioned slippers: the rubber soles were torn and perforated; faded gold embroidery ran along the sides in what looked like a leaping lion motif; and pinned to the back of one of the slippers, a metallic golden sash with words etched into the metal - words that sent shivers down into Bogey's biggest toe.

Farty Bumflump number 1.

The air in the basement was musty, damp and old, and there he stood transfixed, pointing his torch light at the vintage pair of slippers.

'Are you alright down there?' yelled Smell. His voice suddenly startled Bogey, who immediately dropped his rusty old torch and ran back to the hole in the kitchen floor.

'Quick! Get me out of here!' he yelled. 'I want to leave now!'

Smell had found a pair of old stepladders, which Bogey quickly clambered up in a panic. Once he was safely back in the kitchen, he scoured around for any spare pieces of wood and set to work sealing up the hole in the floor.

'I've never seen him work so fast?' puzzled Smell.

'Bogey, what did you find down there?' asked Fluff, looking a little concerned with Bogey's unusual behaviour.

'Things that shouldn't be down there,' said Bogey, banging the last nail into place. 'There, that should do it!' He covered the repaired hole with an old rug, put the kitchen table and chairs on top, straightened the fruit bowl and sat down to rest.

'I didn't know you liked DIY,' giggled Smell.

'I'll make you a cup of tea,' said Fluff, walking over to the teapot.

That afternoon, over tea and out of date biscuits, Bogey told Smell, Fluff and little Crumb who had joined them from next door all about the secret cavern of slippers under their house and the shocking discovery he'd made. Farty Bumflump's original winning slippers from the 1850s. They'd gone missing years ago and hadn't been seen for decades…

'You know, when I was trapped in the Spider's Lair, I found loads of caverns and tunnels under the carpet,' said Crumb with his mouth full. The friendly chocolate chip cookie was trying to swallow a rather mouldy looking Jaffa Cake. 'They led for miles and miles - there must be a maze of passageways under the floorboards.'

'But who would store all those vintage slippers? It makes no sense,' said Bogey, who had turned a pale, mushy-pea green.

'And why are they all under your house?' said Fluff.

'What are you going to do Boges? Are you gonna report it? Remember your race is tomorrow afternoon' said Smell, slightly confused about the whole thing.

'No! Not until I know who is behind this! It could be dangerous and *we* have to live here,' said Bogey, focusing on the cup of tea he'd hardly touched.

That night, after the gale outside had calmed down somewhat, Bogey suggested the friends stay close together, just to be on the safe side. Bogey took his bed, Fluff had Smell's bed and Smell and Crumb slept on the sofa downstairs in the front room.

Smell and Crumb fumbled and fidgeted, trying to get comfy on a very hard and dusty old sofa. The clock in the front room started ticking louder and louder - Smell's eyeballs twitched with every tick it made... An owl twittered from outside in the forest.

'Twitty Poo!' croaked the owl. Also suffering from word flu.

Just then a rustling noise could be heard coming from the kitchen, quickly followed by a muffled smash. Smell instantly stopped breathing…

'Did you hear that?' said Smell, gawping at Crumb.

'Err… I heard the clock ticking and that drunken owl outside… and I can hear munching in me ears again,' Crumb yawned.

'No, the noise from the kitchen! I heard a smash and something being moved,' said Smell. His eyes were wide open.

'I didn't hear that! You sure it wasn't your belly? It's been making some very strange noises since we went to bed.' Crumb chuckled to himself.

'It wasn't my belly! I heard a noise coming from the other room!' Suddenly another muffled smash echoed in the darkness. It was definitely coming from the kitchen.

'I heard that!' said Crumb, sitting bolt upright on the sofa. The hairs on the back of his neck stood to attention and twitched with fright. Smell quietly and very slowly got off the sofa and tip toed toward the door in his underpants. He was sporting his new pair of helicopter underpants that Fluff had bought him for his birthday. He put an ear against the door and stopped breathing for a moment to listen… He could just about hear the gentle tapping of someone walking around in the kitchen. The floorboards creaked very slowly, as if someone was tip towing about. Smell looked at Crumb who had turned a pale shortbread colour. Smell grabbed hold of the kitchen door handle…

'W… what you gonna do?' whispered Crumb, looking spooked.

'I'm going to make a pot of tea!' replied Smell as he slowly turned the handle. It clicked and creaked in the gloomy room as he peered through a tiny gap in the doorway to get a better look. He could definitely hear someone moving around. Without another thought, Smell yanked open the door and leaped into the kitchen, yelling as loud as you like, in his helicopter underpants, his arms waving around like a crazy monkey…

Smell stood in the middle of the kitchen in complete darkness and stopped for a minute to catch his breath. His heart was pumping double-time.

'Who is it?' whispered Crumb, plucking up the courage to peer from behind his pillow.

'Um, I don't know,' whispered Smell, puzzled. He squinted as his eyes adjusted to the gloom of the room. He looked around but could see no one. He listened intensely, but could hear nothing. The kitchen was empty.

'What you mean no one?' said Crumb.

'There's no one in here!' exclaimed Smell as he walked around the kitchen, brandishing Bogey's best teapot like a weapon.

Feeling a little less spooked, Crumb got off the sofa and peered into the room. Just then the staircase in the hallway cracked, footsteps could be heard creaking each floorboard gently. Smell quickly signalled to Crumb to get back and hide whilst Smell scurried like a mouse to conceal himself in the darkness ready to pounce on the intruder. He clutched the teapot tightly and raised it above his head, as the last creaky floorboard bowed with the weight of the prowler. Smell braced himself and then it appeared... Standing in the stairway stood a hideously deformed green monster with an enormous hooter and a ginormous bulging belly. Smell leapt and screamed at the same time, planting the precious teapot onto the grotesque creature's head.

'OW!!!!!' yelled Bogey as he clutched his head in pain. The teapot shattered into hundreds of pieces and scattered across the kitchen floor.

'Boges, what are you doing up?' yelled Smell.

'I heard noises so I came to investigate. What's that you hit me with?'

'Um, nothing... I thought you were a prowler.'

'Wait a minute, I recognise that handle.' Bogey pointed to the broken handle Smell was still clutching.

'That's my favourite...' But before Bogey could get angry a noise from the corner of the kitchen startled them both. Smell immediately sprung back into action, his ears twitching as he scanned the murky room like a cat.

'What was that?' worried Bogey.

'That's what I heard! That's the noise!' said Smell excitedly. Little Crumb quickly scurried back under the blankets in the other room, hoping this was all a dream.

'Look, what's that?' yelled Bogey pointing to the kitchen floor in a panic. Smell grabbed hold of another kitchen utensil, this time a metal saucepan and stared into the corner of the room where the noise had come from.

'It must be a mouse,' thought Smell. 'There's nothing there.' He squinted in the darkness.

'Look on the floor, there's something moving. It's my...' Bogey froze like a statue pointing at something moving on the floor. Smell looked down, but all he could see was a pair of abandoned slippers in the middle of the room.

'That's not like you to leave ya slippers there Boges.'

'I didn't leave them there!' Bogey had gone a pale yellow colour. He didn't look at all well.

Smell looked back at the slippers puzzled... Then, to his astonishment, he witnessed something he had never seen before.

Bogey's brand new pair of Zodiac white stripe slippers, still in their protective wrappings, suddenly started to walk on their own. At first they edged slowly forward and bumped into a chair leg. Then they reversed, turned to their right and walked straight over to the door. The door flung open instantly and the little red and green tartan slippers walked straight out of the house and into the night.

Smell and Bogey stood bemused, staring at each other in the dusky darkness.
'Slippers walking on there own. Whatever next?' pondered Bogey, feeling quite spooked by the ghostly goings on. Smell felt a shiver run down his spine and all the hairs on his arms stood on end. Just then Fluff appeared at the foot of the stairs in her white nightie.
'What's up boys?' she boomed scratching her sleepy head.
The sudden appearance of a white fluffy figure in a white frilly nightie in the middle of the night was enough to make Smell and Bogey jump out of their skin…
AAARRRGGGHHH!!!!

Once the lights in the kitchen had been switched on and everyone had calmed down, Bogey told Fluff and Crumb what had happened to his slippers.
'They were possessed!' cried Smell. 'They were walking on their own with no one in them!' Fluff was sure the boys had been dreaming or chewing on the carpet threads again. The Magic Carpet had potent magical properties and chewing on the threads could

make you hallucinate and do very strange things.

'It's the truth, Fluff! Honest!' said Bogey. 'They walked right out of the kitchen and into the forestt Look - there are slipper prints on the ground!' Bogey pointed to footprints heading across the front lawn and into the darkness. The garden gate had been left open too. The slipper prints headed off into the forest that surrounded Smell and Bogey's little green Monopoly house. The night was full of shadows and a sense of unease found its way into Bogey's tummy.

'I'm going after them!' cried Bogey, suddenly having a burst of inspiration.

'What do you mean Boges? You can't go after them now! It's the middle of the night!' said Fluff. Smell's ears twitched and his toes wiggled with anticipation, the sense of another adventure filled him with excitement.

'I don't care, I'm not having Whiff and Whatnot winning the Carpet Slipper Race for another year! I said I'd beat them and no crazy possessed pair of slippers are gonna stop me! Who's coming?' Bogey stormed upstairs before anyone could answer. Crumb had nodded off into a light snooze, but Smell was standing to attention ready for action.

Upstairs, Bogey found some warm clothing, kitted out a bag with biscuits, cream cakes, a jar of jam and a flashlight and walked back down into the kitchen to rally the troupes. He expected stiff opposition to his crazy midnight walk through the forest, but to his surprise when he got back downstairs everyone was buttoning up warm coats, putting on scarves and hats and making ready. Even Fluff was tying up the laces to her new boots; she had a tendency to blow off at the slightest of gusts so being weighted down by a good pair of boots was a good idea.

'Right then, are we all ready?' said Smell, clapping his hands together.

'Err... hang on one minute boys!' A degree of concern appeared on Fluff's face.

'This is just a recognisance mission. We stay together and if we find the slippers we intercept, apprehend and return to base immediately... understood?'

'Yes ma'am!' said the boys all together. Smell saluted. He was indeed ready for another adventure.

That night, Smell, Bogey, Fluff and a reluctant Crumb headed off into the carpet forest to track down the pair of haunted slippers. The boys marched ahead with a keen eye on the slipper footprints, whilst Fluff cautiously followed behind, realising that every step took them further from the safety of their home.

Chapter Three

Surveillance

'I don't think we should go too far at night guys - you don't know what's lurking in the shadows in the dark.' Crumb looked spooked already, his biscuity-feet had started to crumble.

'We'll get as far as the Twisted Forest and if we haven't spotted the slippers, we'll turn back,' said Bogey, striding out in front with confidence. Fluff looked at Smell and frowned a concerned frown.

'I've heard about strange deformed ghostly creatures that wander the carpet at night. They follow you from behind and pounce when you least expect it,' whispered Smell looking around.

'Shut it Smelly! You'll freak out Crumb even more!' shouted Bogey, putting his arm around the quivering little Hobnob.

'Who's Farty Bumflump?' Crumb asked, hoping it would change the subject.

'An ancient ghost of long ago!' blurted out Smell.

'He's not a ghost! He was the greatest Carpet Slipper Champion of all time!' yelled Bogey, glaring at Smell.

'What happened to him, Boges? Wasn't there a mystery surrounding his disappearance?' asked Fluff, the fluffy hairs on *her* back twitched to attention in the cool night as they walked. Bogey suddenly took a sharp turn to his right then stopped in his tracks. He shone his torch down to the ground, loosing sight of the slipper prints for a moment.

'Farty Bumflump won the Carpet Slipper Race hundreds and hundreds of times back in the olden days. He became a legend and every competitive creature in the Magic Carpet came from miles around to try and beat him, but no one could. Then one year, when he was on course for yet another victory, he vanished completely during a race. He totally disappeared near to the Twisted Forest and was never seen again. A contender by the name of Geraldine Cramp won the race that year… Well, there was talk that she'd bumped him off in order to win. Some say he fell through what we now call Dribble's Leap and others say he was terrified by a gruesome creature deep in the forest and was devoured alive. Weird thing was, Geraldine Cramp disappeared in exactly the same way the year after!'

'Thanks for that, Boges. I'm sure we all feel much more relaxed now!' said Fluff sarcastically.

The night air got colder and colder the deeper they walked. The forest carpet threads had started to change colour from browny orange to redy black, and still no sign of the possessed slippers...

'Have you got your hover-pants with you, Smelly? Just in case we need to make a swift getaway?' enquired Fluff. She suddenly felt a nervous twitch run down her spine, the forest was becoming creepy.

'Yes! Never leave home without them these days,' said Smell confidently.

'Have you heard about Scrag End?' said little Crumb, hoping to lighten the mood.

'No, what's Scrag End?' said Fluff, walking along side the crumbly little biscuit. Each step he took broke off a tiny piece of hobnob from his toes and everywhere he went he left a trail of biscuit crumbs fit for any hungry night dweller.

'Scrag End is where I come from, before Fangs the Spider captured me and cocooned me in his lair.' Fluff put her arm around him: she remembered how they had found him trapped in the spider's lair.

'What's Scrag End like?' asked Smell.

'Um, it's a bit grim to be honest. It's a baron wasteland where all the down and outs end up. It's not a bad old place - it just attracts the strays and the lonely. I don't know how I ended up there.' Little Crumb reminisced about how his life had changed so much since meeting his new wonderful friends. Fluff and

Bogey each had one arm around him as they walked deeper into the forest of carpet.

The Magic Carpet was getting darker and colder. The only light came from Bogey's weakening flashlight, which glowed a dull orange and flickered occasionally. The forest was alive with weird noises and strange rumblings: every snap, crackle and pop made poor little Crumb jump and flinch with fear.

'I think it might be a good idea to stop and wait for morning light,' said Fluff.

'I don't think my batteries are going to last much longer,' worried Bogey, fiddling with his torch. Suddenly the torch light vanished and everyone came to a sudden stop. A girly-scream echoed deep into the carpet forest, coming from Crumb's direction. He really didn't feel comfortable at all. Fortunately, just as soon as the beam had gone out, the flashlight flickered back on again.

'Come on, let's camp here for the night and we can carry on searching at daybreak.' For once in his life, Bogey was completely in charge. His best chum Smell found it quite inspiring to see his friend so confident. Bogey bashed the flashlight and a new burst of power suddenly sprung into life. The beam shone bright, lighting up the whole area…

'Look over there!' screamed Crumb.

Immediately Bogey turned and aimed his torch where Crumb had pointed. To his astonishment, he could see his brand new pair of slippers just standing there, resting. One of the slippers was still covered in its protective wrapping.

'Quick, Bogey! Jump!' yelled Smell. Immediately the possessed slippers sprung into action and started to walk on their own. Bogey dropped his torch in surprise and ran after them. His big, bulging belly bounced up and down, hitting his big enormous hooter and throwing him off course. What a sight! He quickly picked up the torch and shone the beam back into the black forest in front of him.

'Look at that!' yelled Smell who had spotted the slippers moving again. The pair suddenly sprung into action and immediately separated. The left slipper went to the left and the right slipper went to the right and in a blink of an eye they had vanished into the darkness…

'Will you keep it down?! I'm trying to get some sleep!'

'Well you can talk! All I've heard from you tonight is your snoring!'

Smell, Bogey, Fluff and Crumb froze stiff as two new voices echoed in the darkness. Bogey pointed his flickering torch and shone it around in the dead of night. Only the carpet threads stood silent around them like ghostly trees.

'Who was that?' whispered Bogey who had started feeling rather like his old self again, wishing he had never left the comfort of his cosy bed. His knees shook violently with fear.

'Who's that indeed! Who are you? Causing such a commotion at this time of night. I ask you!' The voice came from Bogey's left and sounded gruff and deep but slightly feminine. Then from the right bellowed the second voice. This one was definitely male.

'Aye, clear off the lot of ya or I'll strangle ya with me bare hands!'

'You haven't got any hands, dear,' said the first voice.

'Oh yeah!' mumbled the second voice.

Bogey and friends huddled together for protection. Little Crumb's teeth had started to chatter in time with Bogey wobbly knees.

'We're terribly sorry to have woken you up, but we're a bit lost, see? We're trying to find Bogey's slippers,' said brave little Fluff.

'Bogey's slippers? I ask you! I've never heard such nonsense!' barked the first voice.

'I have! I have to put up with it every blinkin' day from you!' said the second voice.

'Wiggle your flashlight, Boges. Let's see who we're talking to,' said Smell.
Bogey banged the flashlight and then gave it a wiggle. Immediately the light intensified again and shone up into the night sky.

'Hello?' said Smell, puzzled. There was no one around.

'QUIET!' came the first voice. Fluff immediately spotted what was speaking and jumped back in fright falling against one of the carpet threads.

'Oi! Get off will ya!' Fluff was immediately shunted away from the carpet thread. Smell grabbed her arm and pulled her close...

To everyone's amazement, it was two carpet threads that were talking! The left thread was female looking: curvaceous with two large, black eyes hiding amongst woolly fibres. The right carpet thread was butch with muscles and a frowning mouth. They were both attached to the floor but wriggled about when they spoke.

'You're talking?' Smell questioned, taking a closer look at the male one.

'No, I'm not!' bellowed the gruff voice as he leaned over Smell dwarfing him like a giant pipe cleaner.

'Yes you are... you're talking! Look!' Smell pointed at the carpet thread's open mouth.

'That's not me talking! Now scram or I'm gonna get very, *very* angry!'

'You are talking. Your mouth's moving. Look!' Smell challenged the grumpy looking carpet thread.

'Err, can I just jump in at this point. I feel it'll be a long night otherwise!' said the female thread. 'You're right – he is talking but he just likes a good argument. He'll keep on and on and on until you're both blue in the face.'

'So who are you both?' said Fluff intrigued.

'We're long distance lorry drivers and we're trying to get to Belgium!' barked the grumpy one.

'We're the gate keepers to the Twisted Forest, actually,' said the female one.

'That way leads to the Twisted Forest?' quivered little Crumb in horror.

The grumpy one butted in again. 'Yes. And be warned! The two pathways before you will take you on very different journeys. One leads to Hullabaloo and the other leads to certain doom!'

'Hullabaloo?' asked Smell. 'What's Hullabaloo?'

'Could you tell us which is the safe path to take?' asked Fluff politely.

'NOPE! That would be influencing your journey. But you can ask one question and one question only. And remember this… One of us will always tell the truth and the other one will always lie.'

'Only one question?' questioned Bogey.

'Yeah, you got a problem with that?' bellowed the grumpy one as he leaned over Bogey, dwarfing him.

'No, I get it. One question.' Fluff scratched her fluffy head in deep thought. She sat down, crossed her legs and thought hard. Bogey and Crumb both looked very puzzled by the whole thing.

'I think we should go back. It's not worth it just for a pair of slippers,' said Smell. 'We can get you another pair, Boges!'

'No wait, I think I have a question. But we have another problem. The slippers have split up so we're going to have to split up too!' said Fluff.

'But it's dangerous! One way leads to certain doom!' cried Crumb, 'And that sounds dangerous.'

'We've been in the Twisted Forest before and we survived it last time,' Fluff said, standing to attention. She walked over to the female carpet thread.

'If I asked him if the left way was the safe path to take, what would he say?'

Bogey scratched his head, Crumb looked blank and Smell squinted in confusion.

'Yes!' said the female carpet thread positively.

'Right, come on then boys. We're going to have to split up. Bogey and Crumb, you take the right hand lane and Smell and I will take the left one.'

'But which is the dangerous path?' said Crumb.

'It doesn't matter now, we won't go too far. We'll find the slippers and meet straight back here… OK?'

Reluctantly, Bogey and Crumb agreed and took the right path whilst Smell and Fluff headed off on the left path.

Even though it was getting very late, the moonlight had started to shower beams of brilliant white light, cutting the darkness and illuminating the Twisted Forest. Dust swirled and spiralled in the dead of night and if you listened closely, you could hear the strange cries of creatures coming from the darkness.

'What's the Hullabaloo?' said little Crumb as he dragged his feet along the rough weave of the Magic Carpet.

'I think it's the afterlife. Like heaven, you know.' said Bogey, distracted by something up ahead.

'What's the afterlife?'

'It's the place where we all go when we're worm food.'

'Oh, nice.' Bogey suddenly stopped in his tracks and shone his flickering torch straight ahead.

'Why have you stopped?' asked Crumb.

'Look what's out in front of us…' whispered Bogey. His usual greenish complexion was now an unusual white. Crumb peered over Bogey's shoulder and focused on the strange glowing figure that was staring back at them and blocking their way.

'Are you seeking Hullabaloo?' echoed a voice from all around them. It seemed to be coming from the figure in front, but her mouth didn't move. The glowing light around her flickered. The form was most definitely female: an old but pretty face with delicate hazel eyes. She wore a running vest with a jersey tied around her neck, jogging shorts, gleaming white socks pulled up to her knees but, bizarrely, nothing on her feet.

Bogey and Crumb started to inch back slowly, completely spooked.

'Are you seeking Hullabaloo?' asked the voice again. This time the voice seemed to come from inside Bogey's head. Bogey shivered with fright as he yelped out…

'Err, no! We're just after my slippers!' The figure flickered. An empty expression appeared on her face.

'Only those with the purest hearts may enter the Hullabaloo…' echoed the voice again. The spooky figure put out her hands…

'No, that's alright thanks, we're only after my slippers. Sorry to have bothered you.' Bogey started to turn, grabbing little Crumb's hand as he calmly walked away from the creepy creature.

'You *will* be back!' reverberated the voice inside Bogey's mind. Bogey quickly broke out into a run, dragging his crumbly chum behind him.

'Who was that?' enquired Crumb.

'I'm not sure, but I have a funny feeling about all of this and I don't like it one bit.'

'What do you mean?'

'Well first I find a basement full of vintage slippers, then my slippers start to walk on their own and now we're seeing ghostly creatures in the dead of night.' Bogey looked troubled.

'And did you see the clothes she had on? They were really old fashioned...' Crumb had also gone a little pale.

'Yes I know. And if I'm not very much mistaken she was dressed in the old slipper racing outfits from years ago. The sort the professionals used to wear.

'And did you notice how she had nothing on her feet?' cried Crumb.

Before they could go too far, another glowing figure suddenly appeared right before their eyes. It was so close that Bogey didn't have time to stop and he walked straight through the creature.

'*Argh!* YOU ARE NOT ALONE!' yelled Bogey. His voice had suddenly changed for a split second - it was deeper and his eyes bulged as he spoke. He dropped to the floor as the ghostly figure passed by.

'You are not alone! Do you seek Hullabaloo?' said the figure, staring intensely.

This time the figure was male and a lot older than the other one. He was shrivelled and wrinkled and again wearing a running vest, very baggy shorts that reached his down to his knees, glowing white socks pulled up to his knees and, like the figure before, nothing on his feet.

Bogey trembled as he stared at the figure. Again the voice sounded like it was inside their heads. Bogey pulled Crumb close and tried to inch backwards very slowly. This time Bogey knew exactly who the figure before them was. He knew exactly what he was looking at and he didn't like it one bit. Fear travelled down into his big toes and tingled. The night air suddenly went bitter cold as the glowing figure glided closer to them.

'YOU ARE NOT ALONE!' the figure repeated in a creepy voice. Crumb and Bogey froze to the spot in complete dread and fear as they came face to face with the legend of the Carpet Slipper Race.

Farty Bumflump…

Chapter Four

Dribble

'Look, there it is! There!' shouted Smell, pointing at the left slipper. It was still striding ahead with no sign of stopping. Fluff and Smell found it hard to keep up with the freaky footwear. The night had gone cold and the air was crisp. The moonlight shimmered as it reflected off strange objects that stood silently watching, waiting and listening in the shadows. Smell never let on but he felt spooked. Wandering through the Magic Carpet at night, slightly lost and surrounded by the unknown was enough to put the willies up anyone - even the likes of Smell who dreamed about this sort of adventure. Fluff was way out in front and humming a melody to herself.

'What's that you're singing, Fluff?' asked Smell.

'Oh, it's a song I used to sing all the time. I haven't sung it for ages. I don't know why it popped into my head now... It was Dribble's favourite song.' Fluff looked up into the night sky. The tall, woolly threads of carpet stretched upwards, clawing at the sky like fingers. Her eyes glazed over for a minute as memories of her old friend Dribble filled her mind. The song had a melancholy feel to it -

like a nursery rhyme but without any words. Smell walked closer to her and looked into her eyes. He could see the sadness. He smiled and started humming the tune along with her.

Suddenly, Fluff stops in her tracks...

'What's the matter?' said Smell puzzled.

'Look at the slipper!' cried Fluff.

'Where is it?'

'Exactly! I can't see it.' The Magic Carpet was getting very thick and the pathway they were walking had now almost disappeared along with the slipper.

'I can hardly see this deep into the forest, Fluff... Maybe we should stop and wait until things get lighter. We'll have a better chance of following the trail in the daylight,' said Smell, starting to feel a little vulnerable.

'That's a good idea, Smell. We should light a fire and wait until dawn. Let's just hope we can find the slipper in time for Bogey's big race tomorrow.' Fluff had not planned on venturing too far, as *they* were on the path that led to certain doom.

Smell got out his survival kit and made a cosy shelter out of pieces of loose carpet. He managed to get a roaring fire going too. Fluff had brought along some marshmallows and started to roast them over the flame. Smell sat close to Fluff and gazed into the flickering fire. He felt at home and very happy despite their surroundings.

Fluff huddled up next to Smell and handed him a marshmallow. It was blackened on the outside but soft and gloriously gooey on the inside. *Mmmm... Lovely...*

'You know I always feel safe around you Smelly...' Fluff mumbled as she devoured the warm marshmallow. A little dribbled from her mouth.

'Do you? I suppose it's my brave heroic charm,' boasted Smell. The fire flickered and snapped in the chilly night.

'No, not really. I don't know what it is. I just feel content.' Fluff poked at the fire with her stick. There was an awkward silence between the two...

'I'm looking forward to Bogey's big race tomorrow, aren't you?' Smell broke the silence.

'Yes,' sighed Fluff. Smell prodded at the fire.

'I can't wait to see what he looks like in those new slippers and that awful pair of shorts he has to wear. He looks like he's running in his underpants.' Fluff giggled to herself.

'Thank you, Smelly,' she smiled as she lent over and kissed him on the cheek.
Smell smiled and big cheesy smile, slightly embarrassed, not knowing why she had kissed him. The night got colder. Strange noises echoed all around them as Fluff rested her head on Smell's lap.

'Goodnight, Smelly,' she said, closing her eyes.

'Goodnight, Fluffy,' replied Smell, putting his head in his hands... *'Goodnight Fluffy!'* he thought to himself. *'You total berk!'*

Smell had started to nod off. The embers in the fire glowed a deep orange and, despite the night being chilly, Smell felt quite warm with Fluff cuddled up to him. He had a warm content glow coming from his belly. He pondered about Bogey and Crumb for a moment. *'I hope they're alright,'* he thought, remembering that one pathway was supposedly dangerous. His eyelids drew heavy as he laid his chin on his chest to rest...

'Smelly!' came a whisper from the forest, 'Smelly!' it called again.

Smell opened his eyes, startled, not knowing what had woken him. He looked around at the thick, menacing forest that circled him, the tops of the carpet threads swaying in the cold breeze. One of the threads of carpet coughed, putting a single hand to its mouth, while another one yawned and stretched simultaneously, causing several other threads of carpet to yawn back. Smell shivered as he leant towards the dying fire to keep warm.

Suddenly from the other side of the fire appeared a dark splodgey shape. It was changing and re-forming. The fire glowed brighter and hotter. Smell leant back and focused on the strange object before him. He wanted to run but felt glued to the spot by some strange magnetic force. The shape grew and grew, pulsing with the energy from the fire. The dark, blobby shape was changing. It was taking on the form of a figure, a person! Smell could just make out a head, an arm and then eyes and a mouth too. Then before his very eyes it appeared clear as day…

''Ello, Smelly me boy! How the manky old toenails are ya my son?'

Smell just stared in silence with his mouth wide open.

'Well say some thing ya daft old toe-rag! It's bin ages! How ya doin?' said the figure with the smiley face and the big beaming eyes.

'Dribble!' exclaimed Smell. 'You're alive! I can't believe it - you're alive! You survived?'

'Shhh, you'll wake her highness up.' Dribble pointed to Fluff who twitched her nose and turned away from the fire. She was still fast asleep.

'Yes! Let's wake her up, she needs to see you! She misses you so much, Dribble!'

Smell went to wake Fluff up but immediately Dribble yelled at him.

'No!!!! Don't wake her! She can't see me, not like this!' Dribble jumped to his feet and backed away from the fire. The small but toughened creature resembled a teardrop with muscles; a scar ran down his sad face. He gazed at Fluff with affection.

'What do you mean? Dribble, this is Fluff! She has pined and mourned for you for years and now you're here in the flesh! I've got to wake her up. She'll be so happy to see you.'

'No. You mustn't wake her up! She won't be able to see me - only you can see me. Now be quiet or you'll wake her and I need to talk to you.' Dribble paced from left to right with his arms behind his back.

Standing before Smell was the ghostly pale figure of Dribble. Smell couldn't believe his eyes! Dribble hadn't changed a bit. He still looked old and tired, slightly transparent like Smell with his distinctive scar running down his right cheek.

'Well, where have you been? I thought you were dead. I thought you were sucked up with all the fleas?' said Smell bewildered.

'No, no, no me boy! You don't understand see.'

Smell gently rested Fluff's head on the ground and walked over to Dribble.

'What do you mean? I don't understand?' Suddenly the fire flickered and cracked. Dribble's image faded for a moment and then it reappeared.

'Now listen, me boy, I haven't got much time and you are the only one I can talk to about this. I've tried to talk to others, believe me, but you have the gift.'

Smell and Dribble sat by the remains of the fire and talked in a whisper.

'The danger hasn't passed and there's something else on the horizon, something that only you have the power to deal with.' Dribble scratched his head in frustration.

'Me! Why only me?' said Smell.

'I don't know, but if I can talk to you and no one else, then you have some sort of power the others don't have and we need to tap into that ability…'

'But why can't Fluff see you? Or Bogey or Crumb?' Smell scratched his head confused.

'I'm not really here, Smell. *You* shouldn't be able to see me either.'

'But why?' said Smell.

'I'm dead, Smell. I croaked it back at Dribble's Leap all those years ago! I haven't been in a physical form for years. That's why.'

Smell felt a shuddery tingle whizz down his spine. He wanted to move from the spot but he couldn't. He was glued fast. His shoulders felt heavy and paralysed.

'Now do you understand? I don't know why I can only talk to a few, but I think not everyone is connected like you are… And this is why I come to you, see? I can see visions from the future and there is more danger coming. You must get back to your friends fast! Something is here already, waiting, and I can see danger for Fluff too! You shouldn't be out this deep in the Twisted Forest, it's not…'

Suddenly the firelight dimmed again and Dribble's image disappeared in a flash.

'Dribble!' yelled Smell in a panic. Fluff stirred for a moment as she scratched her ear.

'Dribble!' yelled Smell again. The fire glowed a deep orange then a weak vision of Dribble re-appeared.

'I haven't got much energy left, Smell. You must get back to your friends and start to use your powers. You can see like me and hear like me. It's your only hope, Smelly. You must protect Fluff. – don't let her out of your sight! There is great danger - right now!'

Dribble appeared to be distracted for a moment…

'It's a vision…' he announced. 'I can see Fluff and she's trapped. Her mind is taken over by…'

Suddenly a flash of light startled Smell and he too could see the vision. He could see Fluff with no expression on her face. She was cocooned inside a strange white place and surrounded by strands of light. They pulsed like veins which looked like they were feeding off her.

Smell was paralysed to the spot. He looked around in the blinding, deafening white light.

Suddenly he could see another... 'Bogey!' he thought. Bogey was trapped within the veins too.

And then Smell saw himself...

Smell immediately lost his breath and in a blinding flash woke up from the vision. Before him, the dying fire smouldered in the morning light. Fluff was still fast asleep but there was no sign of Dribble anywhere.

'Dribble!' cried Smell. He scanned the area for any sign of life but Dribble had vanished.

The twisted carpet threads twitched and swayed as the morning breeze gathered strength. Smell was confused. He squinted for a moment, thinking he could see something odd clinging to one of the carpet threads way out ahead of him. He shielded his eyes from the wind and focused on one spot. Then he gulped in fear as he reached for his hover-pants scrunched up in his pocket. Two white, piercing eyes stared at him from the other side of the twisted forest. Smell could just about make out the form of a creature hugging one of the carpet threads. The figure seemed camouflaged: it was almost invisible but not completely. Smell quickly put on his hover-pants. Fumbling in a panic, he almost fell as he looked back to catch another glance of the creature, but it had gone.

Smell ran over to Fluff and shook her violently. She woke up with a jolt.

'Quick, Fluff, we've go to get out of here!' He picked up his survival things, grabbed Fluff's arm and started to run in the opposite direction.

'Which way out of here?' he thought to himself. The twisted forest suddenly shuddered all around them, the wind picked up speed and two threads of carpet parted before him, revealing a fresh pathway out in front.

'Quick, run!' yelled Smell. He looked behind him and could see another pair of piercing white eyes staring at them, again clutched to the carpet thread.

As they start to run, the twisted forest opened up before them, forging a new pathway.

'What are we running from?' panted Fluff, becoming out of breath and still in a sleepy daze. Smell looked behind them and could see two more camouflaged creatures clinging to the carpet. Their evil, cat-like eyes were fixated on him. He quickly changed direction and immediately the twisted forest opened up another new pathway before him. They ran faster and faster but Smell could see a pair of eyes way out in front staring back. He quickly jumped right and instantly the twisted forest opened up. But it was no use. More eyes staring back, there were eyes everywhere! Fluff suddenly let out a high-pitched yelp as she too noticed the malevolent eyes before them.

'What are they, Smell?'

'I don't know. But they're not friendly whatever they are,' replied Smell, looking for another direction to take. Fluff looked down and noticed Smell was wearing his hover-pants.

'Use your hover-pants, Smelly!' she cried.

'Oh yes, I forgot I had them on! Quick, hold on to me tight!' Fluff flung her arms around Smell and held on for dear life. she squeezed him tight as Smell held his breath and instantly they shot up high in to the air, far above the twisted forest and into the hazy morning mist. Fluff let out another yelp, this time in excitement.

'Oh wow! This is so cool, Smelly!' She looked down to take in the view but couldn't see a thing,

'It's too misty!' Smell suddenly blurted out a gusty breath of air and instantly they fell back down toward the carpet.

'Hold on!' yelled Smell as he caught his breath. Just then another vision appeared in his mind. A vision of Bogey's slipper! It was deep in the Twisted Forest surrounded by tatty threads of carpet…

'Take me there!' he cried out loud. Immediately, something took control of the hover-pants and in a flash Smell and Fluff were back on land and stood right in front of the thing they'd been searching for - Bogey's left slipper.

'How did you do that?' cried Fluff in astonishment.

'I don't know… I had a vision of the slipper so I said *Take me there*' and we arrived here.' The slipper was now dormant, surrounded by thick twisted forest but instead of the usual reds, browns and oranges, the carpet threads were grey, white and black - they seemed to be covered in a strange white dust.

'What is it?' asked Smell. Fluff reached out to touch the snowy trees.

'It's some sort of fluffy fluff covering the carpet,' said Fluff as she played with a piece she'd broken off. It was sticky to the touch and it crumbled.

'Ooh, it's weird! It tingles,' she said as she rubbed her hands clean.

'It's Bogey's slipper all right. Look! Number thirteen.' Smell pointed at Bogey's race number printed on the back. Suddenly, the slipper sprung into life again and started to walk on its own. It strode ahead, trying to navigate through the thick forest. Smell immediately jumped onto the feisty footwear and grabbed it with both hands.

'Got it!' he yelled.

'Oh well done, Smelly-pants! Now we can head back. We've still got time before Bogey's big race.'

Smell put on Bogey's slipper, picked up his survival bag and, with Fluff on his arm, walked back through the Twisted Forest in the morning sunshine. They had a spring in their step satisfied at their success, but Smell was puzzled.

How could slippers walk by themselves, he thought to himself. What were those creatures in the forest? And why was Dribble able to communicate with him? Fluff took hold of Smell's hand and smiled her pretty smile, which would normally melt Smell instantly, but he still felt troubled…

Chapter Five

Scrag End

'Why do we get into these situations?' thought Bogey as he tried to run through the thick Twisted Forest pulling little Crumb behind him. 'I'd love to be doing some polishing. I bet the house is in a right state!' he grumbled to himself.

'I think it's gone, Boges,' said Crumb, catching a glance from behind.

The pair had been running for so long the morning sun was now shining onto the Magic Carpet. Bogey kept replaying in his mind the last words the ghostly figures had said… *'You are not alone!'* And despite planning it for ages, his big slipper race was far from his mind.

The Twisted Forest had started to thin out. The pathway had widened and all around them lay bits of old tat and rubbish strewn on the ground: a piece of old bicycle chain; a red Lego building brick; the head of a yellow bath duck and what looked like green goo dripping from the tops of the carpet threads. Suddenly, from behind them, a stranger appeared. Bogey jumped with fright. Pale and lifeless, the figure walked straight past Bogey and Crumb and carried on ahead, not noticing them at all.

'Morning!' yelled Bogey sarcastically, waving one arm in the air. 'Friendly round here, aren't they?' Crumb looked up at Bogey, puzzled.

'What's that smell?' Crumb covered his nose with his hands. Immediately, another figure walked past them, this time walking straight between them both.

'Oi!' yelled Bogey. The figure was tall and lanky - he looked like an old piece of pipe cleaner. His body was wiry and his face vacant with no expression. He ignored Bogey and Crumb and walked on, disappearing to the right.

'Let's follow him, Crumb,' said Bogey, starting to get fed up with being ignored.

'Shouldn't we be looking for your slipper? Your big race is this afternoon and we still haven't found it.' Crumb scratched his head, causing a little piece of chocolate chip cookie to crumble to the floor.

'Ooh, elevenses! Good idea - I'm starving.' Bogey picked up Crumb's crumbly bits and munched on them with delight, his belly growled with hunger pains.

'Oi! That's cannibalism!' shouted Crumb.

'No it's not - it's lunch! I'm not a Crumb. And besides, I'm starving. Mmmm... you're lovely, Crumb. Very tasty.' Crumb took one step back and started to feel very nervous around his big-bellied chum.

Bogey and Crumb carried on walking in the general direction of the two strange figures. As they turned the corner, the Twisted Forest threads suddenly opened up, revealing a new pathway before them.

'It really unnerves me when they do that,' said little Crumb, looking up at the carpet tops.

'ARE YOU SURE YOU WANT TO GO THIS WAY?' exclaimed a number of voices coming from above. The Magic Carpet rumbled with the noise.

Bogey and Crumb looked up to see the carpet tops sway in the morning breeze.

'Who's that?' Bogey cried, feeling helpless. Crumb inched nearer to his friend, again grabbing Bogey's arm.

'Come on, Crumb. There's no one there. No one brave enough to say that face to face any how!' Bogey shouted up at the carpet tops. He was definitely getting used to all this adventure and becoming quite confident. Suddenly, all the carpet threads wriggled and swayed...

'I'LL GIVE YOU BRAVE !' shouted the voices again. There were lots and lots of different voices: female voices; male voices; old voices; young voices; silly voices; and moody voices, all talking at the very same time. It was quite confusing.

Just then, a half eaten orange flew at them, bounced onto the ground and squirted little Crumb in the face.

'Quick!' yelled Bogey, grabbing Crumb's hand. 'Run!' As they ran, the twisted carpet threads opened up before them revealing a new pathway every time.

SPLAT! went a giant half eaten cough sweet. Syrup and gunge oozed out of the lemony shell and splatted Bogey in the face.

'Ooooh! It's hot! It's burning! Get it off!' he yelled, wiping his eyes in pain.

As they ran from the low flying objects including apple pips, sharp bits of toenail-clippings and several dried up lumps of phlegm, Bogey looked up to see hundreds of carpet threads screaming and shouting, flinging what looked like arms around in anger. From behind, Crumb heard a rustling noise. He quickly turned around to see another strange figure right behind him. His face was blank and he looked possessed as he walked straight past Bogey and Crumb.

'Quick, follow him!' yelled Bogey. The figure was very pale, he held his hands out in front of him as he mumbled to himself. He was following a mouldy patch of carpet that carved its way through the forest like a snowy white pathway. Just then, a figure they'd seen before appeared and behind him was another familiar figure. They were all following the trail and all of them looked like they were sleepwalking.

'Do you really think following them is a good idea, Boges? They look pretty freaky to me…' said Crumb.

'Well it's either this or get squished by a low flying object!' Bogey stayed close to the tallest freaky figure as they followed the white, mouldy pathway deeper and deeper into the Twisted Forest.

'Listen. I can here someone!' exclaimed Bogey, pricking up his fat green ears. Crumb gawped to listen. A distant shouting could be heard coming from the other side of the forest. Bogey and Crumb sped up. The pale figures were way out in front and walking on the mouldy white pathway – they were now the same colour as the trail, which seemed to be leading them straight towards the shouting…

Just then, the Twisted Forest opened up before them, revealing a vast open space in the Magic Carpet. Bits of debris lay scattered all over the place. Dust plumes swirled in the morning haze as phlegm piles dribbled to the ground from the carpet tops above. A number of downtrodden creatures wallowed aimlessly, dragging their feet. Some were picking their noses whilst others were trying to climb the threads of carpet only to fall back down to the ground with a bump. Some were so bored they'd resorted to eating phlegm piles for breakfast. Screams and groans could be heard from all around and a sense of gloom filled the stale air. The mouldy white pathway was spreading all over the Magic Carpet: it was growing off the carpet threads, spreading across the floor and eating away at the people too. Some had arms covered in mould, whilst others had white mouldy feet or hands…

'Reach for the skies, mister!' came a soft but gruff voice.

Bogey and Crumb immediately raised their hands in the air in defeat, looking around to see where the voice had come from…

'This town ain't big enough for the both of us Hiccup!' shouted another voice from the other side of the field.

'So what you gonna do about it Burp? You think you can just breeze in here and take over our town?'

'Yep! That's what I intend to do.' The second voice was older and more aggressive than the first.

'Well ask yourself one question, punk… Do you feel lucky? Well do ya, punk?' said the first voice.

Suddenly, gunfire broke out and echoed far into the depths of the Magic Carpet. Bogey and Crumb dropped to the floor and covered their ears in pain. Bogey looked up still confused as to where all this commotion was coming from.

'There, look. Over there!' Crumb pointed to the other side of the forest where two carpet dwellers were standing but one of them was falling to the floor clutching his stomach.

'Wait a minute, I recognise this place,' yelled Crumb excitedly.

'What do you mean? said Bogey.

'This is my old home... This is Scrag End! What's happened to the place?'

Suddenly another gunshot fired but this time the shot came whizzing toward Bogey and Crumb.

'Duck!' yelled Bogey as they both drop to the floor again...

'Reach for the skies or I'll blow you to kingdom come!' Bogey and Crumb immediately put their hands into the air. Little Crumb couldn't keep his arms still with fright. Then, what looked like a cowboy slowly walked into view, spurs jangling as he walked calmly towards the helpless friends. The glare of the morning sunlight hid the stanger's face. He wore a large brimmed hat so wide at least three men could shelter from the rain under it, a stripy waistcoat, crocodile skin cowboy boots and he held two fingers out in front, pointing them like pistols. As he got closer the smell of tobacco wafted up Bogey's nose. The cowboy stopped and stared down at the quivering couple.

'Well what have we here?' the cowboy said as he spat out a slimy black slop from his mouth. It landed very close to Crumb. Just then the cowboy coughed an enormous girly cough and spluttered and struggled to catch his breath. Bogey looked up for a second to take a closer look, and frowned for a moment...

'It's a girl,' he whispered to little Crumb who was waiting for it all to end.

'And they aren't pistols, they're fingers!' he whispered.

'Get up and face me man to man!' growled the cowboy.

Bogey and Crumb slowly stood up with their hands still raised in the air and came face to face with the cowboy's fingers.

'Excuse me, are they loaded fingers?' Crumb asked politely.

Just then the cowboy yelped out what sounded like gunfire. The sound was deafening and very realistic, but it came from his mouth not his loaded fingers. Crumb instantly fainted and fell to the floor while Bogey flinched closed his eyes and waited for the end to come.

'Hiccup! Hiiiiiccup! Your breakfast's ready, it's getting cold! Come on in and wash your hands!' came a mumsy voice from the edge of the forest.

'Oh, just five more minutes... perrrlease!' shouted the cowboy. This time his voice was positively girly. Crumb woke up, squinted and looked up at the prettiest cowboy he'd ever seen.

'You're a girl!' he yelled, pointing at the very pretty face before him. She had big dark dreamy eyes, rosy pink cheeks and the cutest little nose.

'Hiccup, get in now or else!' came the mumsy voice again.

'Sorry chaps, I'm awfully sorry but I'm gonna have to dash, but give me ten and I'll be back out to play I promise. Auntie's a stickler for punctuality at the breakfast table.' And in a flash and a jangle of her spurs, she was gone.

'Wow! What a girl,' sighed Crumb, looking all dreamy and starry eyed.

'What's up with you?' asked Bogey looking around at Scrag End. The place was desolate and very baron.

'She's wonderful… Don't you think she's dreamy?' Crumb stood up and sniffed the air where she had stood and sighed.

'Pull yourself together, crumbly boy! One glance of a girl dressed as a cowboy with loaded fingers for pistols and you go all gooey on me? I asked you!' Just then, Bogey noticed the mouldy white pathway that lead right through the centre of Scrag End and out the other side. The mould had started to creep its way over everything. Suddenly, someone moved. Bogey nudged Crumb, who was still sniffing the air.

'Look, another one!' He pointed to a figure getting up off the floor on the far side of Scrag End. The weird creature looked over at Bogey and Crumb and started to walk toward them.

'Quick! Put your hands up again, Boges,' said Crumb.

'What's he gonna do - tickle us to death with his loaded fingers? They're all barking mad round here if you ask me,' mumbled Bogey.

The small figure hobbled closer. He was limping and dragging something behind him.

'What's up with him?' Crumb whispered.

'I don't know but look what he's dragging behind him!'

As the pitiful creature wobbled into view, large droopy eyes looked up at Bogey and Crumb. The treetops of the forest fidgeted and twitched as the figure dragged behind him a yarn of white mould. It stretched as he walked nearer. The yarn was attached to the pathway of mould and tentacles had started to grow out from the fluffy growth. They wriggled like worms in soil. Bogey looked around to see the whole of Scrag End being devoured by this strange white stuff. Everything was turning mouldy.

'Are you OK?' said little Crumb, putting his hand out to steady the creature.

'Don't touch me... *BURP!*' burped the sad figure.

'What's your name?' asked Bogey.

BURP! went the creature, the whole of his body shuddering with the sound of the burp. He looked just like a burp, or a prickly hedgehog with a big smile and huge friendly eyes.

'Burp's your name?' asked Bogey again.

BURP! yelled the creature as he nodded.

'What's happened to you?' asked Crumb.

'I've been infected. Tell Hiccup I'm infected... *BURP!*' Suddenly, he collapsed on the ground and bent his head in exhaustion. The white mould has started to creep up his left arm and parts of his toes were covered as well.

'Infected by what?' cried Bogey.

'I don't know - *BURP!* - what it is, but everyone's getting it. The white stuff crawled out from the forest last week and ever since - *BURP!* - people have been turning into zombies and leaving Scrag End!'

'Where do they go?' asked Crumb, taking one step back.

'We don't know. But they're never seen again. Hiccup's dad was one of the first to get - *BURP!* - infected. He just walked into the Twisted Forest and we haven't seen him since.'

'This is weird,' said Bogey, scratching his head. 'First my slippers, then the ghosts in the Twisted Forest and now this! There's definitely something whiffy going on around here.'

After a breakfast of stale biscuits and cold tea provided by Hiccup's auntie, the three sat beside Burp trying to comfort him the best they could. Crumb had gone all dreamy again at the sight of Hiccup whilst Bogey tried to figure out what to do.

'Smell would have an idea,' he thought, hoping his two friends were OK.

'I think we should get back to the Carpet Arena and let everyone know the danger. The white mould might spread through the entire carpet,' said Bogey.

'What's the arena?' asked Hiccup.

'I'm supposed to race today in the Carpet Slipper Race. Everyone gathers for the racing in the arena. You should come and watch - it's a huge spectacle.'

'Oh yes. I'd like that!' said Hiccup.

'Just think, Boges. If you hadn't lost your slippers, we might not have met Hiccup,' drooled Crumb.

'You've lost your - *BURP!* - slippers?' burped Burp. The white stuff had now covered both his arms and was creeping up his neck too.

'Yes, we were looking for them in the forest. They were walking on their own last time we saw them!' said Crumb.

'They lead us here!' said Bogey.

'I've seen them! *BURP!* Well, one of them!' Burp suddenly sprang up and retraced his footsteps back to the other side of Scrag End.

'Be sure not to touch the white stuff! That's how you get infected!' shouted Hiccup.

Hiccup, Bogey and Crumb had followed Burp to where he had seen Bogey's slipper. Crumb suddenly steadied himself - the mould was crawling everywhere and tentacles were wriggling, grabbing hold of anything that came near. It wouldn't be long before the whole of Scrag End was completely covered in mould.

'Over there!' yelled Burp, pointing to the other side of the mouldy pathway. The threads of Magic Carpet creaked and cracked as mouldy tentacles tightened their grip. On the other side of the pathway sat one lonesome slipper, just sitting there resting on its own.

'How we gonna get that?' yelled Hiccup.

'Right watch this. *BURP!*' cried Burp, taking a few steps back. He ran as fast as his little legs would carry him and sprung into the air. He flew, then glided like a butterfly, gracefully and elegantly, or as gracefully and elegantly as a burp could glide. He let out an enormous belch at the top of his voice as he flew on the breeze.

BUUUURRRRPPPP!!!!

Suddenly, the mouldy pathway below wriggled and bubbled like a raging river. Then, with an almighty eruption, it sprung into life and three long, hairy, white tentacles leapt up and grabbed both his legs. Burp immediately fell to the ground, wriggling to get free from their tightening hold. But it was no use. The more he struggled, the tighter the tentacles gripped him.

'Burp!' yelled Hiccup with fright. Bogey and Crumb could only watch as their new little friend was pinned to the ground.

'I'm OK... I think... I can reach it!' Burp stretched out to try and reach Bogey's slipper and with a fingertip managed to touch it.

'Quick, throw it over and we'll try and free you!' shouted Bogey, moving an inch nearer to the pathway.

'Watch out!' said Crumb. The pathway was writhing and wriggling with excitement near Bogey's toes. Burp threw the slipper over to Bogey and it landed at his feet. He slipped his foot into it. It fitted him like a glove. No, like a slipper.

'Oh well done Burp! It's my slipper alright. It's the perfect fit.' Bogey proudly paraded up and down with one slipper on his foot.

'Right then, let's try and free you now!' he yelled over at Burp.
But Burp was now standing up right. His hands were by his sides; he stared at Hiccup with a tear in his eye and a blank expression on his face.

'Burp, you're free!' Hiccup shouted, reaching out with her hands.

Burp just stood in silence, now completely covered in the white stuff…

'Oh no,' whispered Hiccup. She covered her mouth with her hands.

Burp broke free from the mouldy tentacles and started to walk on the decaying, mouldy pathway in front.

'Get off it Burp, please!' Hiccup tried to follow him but Bogey and Crumb stopped her just in time. Burp walked straight past them in a complete trance and followed the mouldy pathway into the Twisted Forest. The carpet threads parted as he vanished into the gloom.

'Burp! Burp! Come back! Don't leave me!!!' screamed Hiccup. Her pretty eyes filled with tears as she fell to the ground and sobbed.

The Magic Carpet Map

83

Chapter Six

Whiff and Whatnot

'Well it sure is a perfect day for the Carpet Slipper Race, ladies and gentlemen,' announced Heron on the tannoy back at the arena. 'We have record attendance this year and after yesterday's spectacular opening ceremony, today's racing promises to be nail-biting stuff.'

'Yes indeed... *HICCUP!* hiccupped Finch, 'And I *have* been told that Mrs Mite, mother of Gnarl and Barkley, has in fact nibbled off all her fingernails in the excitement and is now starting on her toenails.' The two fleas were back in their commentary box ready for the days racing, a huge crowd had gathered, decorating the arena with every colour of the rainbow.

Just then, the day's main competitors walked into the arena. An enormous cheer erupted as they waved at the crowd. Each contender wore different brightly coloured jerseys and multi-coloured hats. Strolling out in front was Fangs and his little son Legs wearing his four pairs of brand new slippers: Zodiac Flash - they flashed in the morning sunlight as the cheering got louder. The two dust mites - Gnarl and Barkley, from south of the Magic Carpet - followed them. They were dressed in their family hand-knitted jerseys, small hairy legs protruded and their eyes were fixed in a frown. Mrs Mite waved with such pride at her two boys. Then a few slightly stranger looking creatures entered, all waving at the crowd. An enormous long Millipede crawled into the arena, with millions and millions of slippers on its millions and millions of legs.

'Boy oh boy!' announced Heron. 'You don't get many millipedes entering the Carpet Slipper Race, so we are truly honoured to welcome Malcolm today!'

'Yes, his slipper bill must be GYMOUNGOUS!' agreed Finch.

'It must take him days to put on all those slippers!' giggled Heron.

Behind Malcolm came a very odd sight indeed. A ball of woolly, fluffy fuzziness rolled into view. He didn't walk - he rolled and every now and again a pair of legs would appear sporting a pair of tatty old carpet slippers. The soles were peeling off and the pattern was faded.

'Another new edition to this year's race, ladies and gentlemen, is Woolly Wumpa!' Heron pointed at the fuzzy ball of fluff with no head. He whizzed around looking slightly confused. A few giggles came from the crowd as Woolly Wumpa tried to make his way to the starting position.

Suddenly, the crowd's cheering intensified, while some even booed as two familiar creatures made their way into view. The Carpet Slipper Champions Whiff and Whatnot entered the arena. They walked straight to their starting blocks and started to limber up, not once acknowledging the crowd.

'Come on, Whiffy! Win for us, Whatty!' shouted two female fans in the crowd. They were both wearing specially printed T-shirts: one read *"Whiff"* and the other read *"Whatnot"*.

The atmosphere was electric: all sorts of carpet dwellers from all walks of life had gathered to watch the racing. The colourful bunting flapped in the warm morning breeze as

Mr Mayor, sporting a bright red and very soar nose, wobbled up to the Magic Carpet flag in the centre of the arena. Everyone was very excited.

Suddenly, a fanfare boomed out from the tannoy and everyone stood to attention and bowed their head in respect. Slowly but surely, eight tiny little Soldier Ants bent over in agony wheeled out the enormously flabby and very wobbly bulk that could only be... the Queen of the Ants. Everyone immediately applauded - streamers flew through the air and balloons were released into the blue sky. Flabby layers oozed and wobbled over fatty layers as the Queen inched into view very slowly. She waved regally with one hand, whilst another hand stuffed her face with fruitcake covered in lashings of extra thick double cream.

SPLAT! went one of the not–so-strong Soldier Ants as his legs buckled under the enormous pressure.

'Oooohh! Poor fella!' announced Finch.

'Lemons and Mentlegen,' spluttered the Mayor of the Magic Carpet in the centre of the arena. 'Insects, creatures and thingy me bobs... Welcome to the forty-ninth Carpet Slipper Race. Let the games begin!'

A deafening roar of cheering reverberated around the arena as Whiff and Whatnot line up with the other contenders ready for the first race of the day.

At the starting ribbon gathered Blobs and Splodges, Fuzzballs and Farts, Ants and Mites, Spiders and Thingy-Me-Bobs, all dressed in their racing colours and all wearing carpet slippers on their feet. Whiff turned to Whatnot and whispered something into his ear. Then the starting marshal appeared holding his starting gun, the white ribbon was held up tight, the contenders crouched into their starting positions and then…

BANG!!!!!!

They're off!

Well, team Whiff and Whatnot were.

Whiff leapt into the lead straight away, his dangly long hairs trailing from his nose flap in the wind as he sped along as fast as he could. Round and round the arena track he flew.

'Look at Whiff go!' shouted Heron over the tannoy.

'Go Whiffy!' shouted Whatnot from the starting grid. He chuckled to himself quietly as he looked around at the commotion that had broken out on the starting line.

'Ooooh dear! What *has* happened, ladies and gentlemen?' Heron announced, looking puzzled.

'The Carpet Slipper Champion is way out in front!' shouted Finch. 'He's developing an enormous lead, Herron, but what is up with the other contenders?'

All the other runners were still on the starting grid and going nowhere: no one could get off their starting blocks. Dust Mite Gnarl struggled, the ant team all struggled.

'BOOO!' yelled the Queen of the Ants, whilst she tucked into a live hot dog.

Yelp! went the hotdog.

The Woolly Wumpa struggled, Malcolm the Millipede struggled; there were legs and feet all over the place! He'd left the starting blocks all right but all his slippers had stayed behind - all one million of them were stuck fast! He was very upset indeed.

Everyone seemed to be stuck to the starting blocks. The starting marshal walked over to inspect the Woolly Wumpa's pair of slippers. He looked closely and tried to lift his feet off the track, but they wouldn't budge an inch. The starting marshal checked all the contenders' slippers and then made a sign to Heron and Finch in the commentary box.

'I can't believe it, ladies and gentlemen!' announced Heron in shock. 'This has to be the first time ever in the history of the Carpet Slipper Race that we've got a winner before the race has even finished. Ladies and gentlemen, the winner of the first race today, all the way from the Twisted Forest, it's the reining Carpet Slipper Champions... Whiff and Whatnot!'

The crowd booed and jeered in disapproval. Whiff was now miles away, still racing away deep in the Magic Carpet. Finch shook his head in confusion and disbelief and the Queen of the Ants shouted something unrecognizable - her mouth was full of cream cake, live hot dogs, roasted toenail clippings and not to mention the whole bag of snotty floss on sticks that she'd just devoured.

After a lot of commotion, gossiping, debating and waffling, it was announced to the crowd that the first race had indeed been won by team Whiff and Whatnot. The crowd did not like it at all. The other contenders threw their brand new slippers into the air in disgust, Malcolm the Millipede stormed off in a huff and the Woolly Wumpa was sobbing in the corner and being comforted by the Queen who'd accidentally dribbled tomato sauce over his head.

'I have never known it, Finch,' said Heron. 'The first race of the forty-ninth Carpet Slipper Championship and someone has glued the other contenders' slippers to the starting blocks!'

'I just can't believe it, Heron. *HICCUP!* Who would do such a thing?' Finch shook his head as he looked around the arena. The crowd jeered as the Mayor and his wife walked onto the podium in the centre of the arena to try and calm the hostile mob.

'Mumbles and Fancymen!' the Mayor cried out, still suffering from his word flu. 'I will endeavour to fiddle with the flip-flops before any butties are too hairy. You mark my burgers!' He twiddled his bright red hooter with a hanky.

'*BOOOO!!!!*' shouted the disgruntled crowd, as a rogue tomato whizzed through the air, passing dangerously close to Mrs Mayor.

Whatnot was now busy polishing Whiff's spare pair of slippers. He was very pleased with the outcome indeed.

After a fine demonstration from the ladies acrobatics display team, choreographed by Mrs Fangs and her girls with the lovely legs, which entertained and calmed the crowd down somewhat, Heron and Finch announced the start of the next race.

'Ladies and gentlemen, I'm getting reports that Bogey and Smell's team have *still* not registered for this year's event!' A gasp reverberated around the crowd. 'But I'm sure Bogey will be racing this afternoon.' The crowd mumbled and rustled with their betting sheets. 'We have a spectacular race lined up for you next though. Don't we, Finch?'

"Yes, indeed. *HICCUP!*' said Finch. 'It's the race we've been looking forward to. After his heroic performance during the uprising of the Fleas, everyone has been talking about Fangs and this is his opportunity to really show us what his family are made of. It's the first ever entry of a spider in the Carpet Slipper Race. Ladies and gentle – *HICCUP!* Please welcome Fangs' youngest son... Legs!'

The crowd erupt into a frenzied roar. Banners waved, children jumped and screamed, grannies fainted and babies dribbled. Fangs had become quite a local hero in the Magic Carpet and everyone was delighted to see little Legs walk into the arena escorted by his father. Mrs Fangs waved four of her long legs in the air. Her eight big black eyes sparkled with pride.

Alongside Legs, the strangest looking contenders fidgeted and limbered up ready for the next race: there were blobby ones and thin ones, smelly ones and silly ones. Their trainers gave them last minute words of encouragement as the starting marshal appeared once again with his starting gun.

Just then, the ground began to rumble. Then it began to shudder. Then it began to tremble. Then it began to bounce. The whole arena wobbled with the vibration and then on the horizon appeared an enormous orange fluffy sight. For a moment the sunlight was blocked out by its immense size and then…

'HELLLLLLLLOWW!!!' came the deep and dopey voice. Two enormous brown eyes and a speckled nose looked down on the arena.

'Ladies and gentlemen,' announced Heron with excitement, 'we are honoured to be joined by Gingerbags the Cat!' Everyone waved and cheered.

'OHH, DIDDLEY MIND ME. I WAS JUST PASSING BY AND I THOUGHT I'D CONGRIDDLEY-TATE THE WINNER. WHO *HAS* WON BY THE WAY?' Gingerbags the cat was enormously big, immensely fluffy, hugely ginger and very cuddly but unfortunately a little bit dim. He often slept by the fireplace south of the Magic Carpet and would pop by now and then to see his small friends.

'Err, no one's won yet, Gingerbags,' said Finch over the tannoy. 'We should have our champion later this afternoon though!'

'OH. IN THAT CASE, I'LL JUST FLUMP ME-SELF DOWN 'EAR FOR A WIDGET OR TWO!' Gingerbags curled up into and giant fluffy ginger ball and yawned a gigantic ginger yawn. Suddenly, all the air in the Magic Carpet was momentarily sucked into his massive ginger mouth and then... everyone fell asleep!

Mr and Mrs Mayor were out like a light. They flopped onto the ground and fell fast asleep with their legs in the air. Heron and Finch in the commentary box passed out in front of their microphones and both began to snore very, *very* loudly! The tannoy picked up the snoring and reverberated the noise all around the arena. The whole place rumbled and shook with the sound. Most of the spectators fell asleep in their seats and began to dream and all the contenders who were limbering up ready for the next race immediately passed out on their backs and began to dribble like babies. What a sight!

When people eventually started to come around from their afternoon snooze, only a few of the contenders were lively enough to race. The starting marshal, still half asleep, fired his starting gun. His gun went off but he was pointing it at the ground instead of in the air. 'OWE!' He yelled as he shot his big toe. 'OWE OH OWE!!!!' The shot had certainly woken him up.

Mrs Fangs had poured lashings of hot coffee from her thermos. Little Legs and his father had managed to drink several cups and were now bouncing up and down like kangaroos on a trampoline. When little Legs heard the gunfire, he leapt from the starting grid and flew! The only other contenders awake enough to race were so drowsy that they ended up wandering off the course and were immediately disqualified. Thankfully most of the audience were still fast asleep and too busy dreaming to care.

Finally, Heron and Finch woke up. Heron had fallen asleep with his mouth wide open and Finch's enormous nose had somehow made its way into Heron's mouth.

'EURRGGGHHH! GET IT OUT!' Heron yelled in disgust. Finch immediately woke up with a jolt and looked even more confused than normal.

Once they'd realised what had happened, Heron and Finch started to yell as loud as they could into their microphones to encourage the audience to wake up.

The noise was completely deafening. Louder and LOUDER and LOUDER they both screamed! *Will there ever be any racing today?*

Chapter Seven

Drunk

Once the audience had woken up and the starting marshal had bandaged his injured foot and plied the next race contenders with extremely strong coffee, Heron and Finch set about announcing the next race.

'Ladies and gentlemen!' yawned Heron. 'I promise you we *will* see some great racing today and the next race in the main arena is a very special race indeed!'

'That's right, Heron,' said Finch. '*HICCUP!* The third race of the day is set aside for our brave protectors of the Magic Carpet. Please give a warm welcome to our Magic Carpet soldiers... The Ant Army!!' Suddenly the crowd went wild and screamed. Flags were waved with enthusiasm and the older generation in the audience stood up and saluted with pride. The Ant Army band struck up and out into the arena they marched. Drummers drummed, trumpeters trumped and horn blowers got very excited as they marched into view. Ten little black ants filed in perfect time with their music, each one playing an instrument and wearing the Ant Army colours of scarlet and gold. Leading out in front was the new leader of the ants, Lord Twitching, who gazed nobly at the crowd as they marched in time. He was tall, handsome and strong – the perfect specimen of an Army Ant. The Queen of the Ants suddenly became very excited, jiggling up and down on her royal chaise longue. The poor little fellas who supported her below started to tremble, then they started to wobble and then... the Queen and her royal settee fell to the floor with an almighty *THUD!* Cakes, scones and jam rolls went flying into the air and six brave little ants went... *SPLAT!!!* Lord Twitching immediately stopped his men in the procession and saluted with pride as the band played a quick rendition of the Last Post as a mark of respect. He paused for a second and bowed his head. His scarlet cloak trailed behind him and his face was almost completely covered by the most enormous moustache you have ever seen! It was so big, he had to pin it up into a fancy arrangement in order to see where he was going.

'The Ant Army have been training intensely for the last six months,' said Heron, 'and Lord Twitching has said that his men are in perfect condition and ready to take on anyone who challenges their superior form!'

'That's fighting talk. *HICCUP!*' said Finch. 'But will they manage to get off the starting line? That's proved to be today's biggest challenge so far!'

The crowd jeered and waved their flags in the air, desperate for some sporting action. The ants were the embodiment of pure dedication and might in the Magic Carpet: they were noble and proud creatures and would lay down their lives to save their Queen. All ten ants were now in their starting position and ready to race, each wearing a different coloured jersey and a brand new pair of carpet slippers. Muscles flinched, antennas twitched and heads were held high, their minds focused on one thing and one thing only - winning!

WHOOOOSH!!!! went the door to the spare room, where the Magic Carpet lay. Into the room walked Mum, clutching an enormous glass of deliciously fruity red wine. She was wearing a very posh evening dress, which glistened in the afternoon sunlight.

'I think it's in the toy box!' she yelled to someone downstairs. Someone downstairs mumbled something back at her.

'Are you sure? I thought Liam had it last… When we were on holiday in Wales!' she yelled again resting her glass of Merlot on the bedroom dresser. She opened the gigantic toy box, revealing hundreds of children's toys and games and started to rummage. The voice from downstairs mumbled something else. Mum bolted upright.

'Oooh, I know where it is now. I put it in the bottom drawer of the dresser. It was the day Nan was round last, you remember? She wanted to check it hadn't been damaged so I wrapped it up in old blankets.' Mum bent down and reached out to open the bottom draw of the dresser. She tugged at the handles but the draw was jammed tight. She tugged again, but still the draw would not open. Another jerk but the drawer wouldn't budge an inch. Determined not to be beaten, Mum got into a good position, feet wide apart, bent over in her posh evening dress and got ready to yank with all her might.

'One... two... three... PULL!' She pulled, tugged, jerked and yanked all at the same time. Immediately, the bottom dresser drawer slid open, sending mum flying backward. She let go of the handles and landed on her bum with her feet in the air. She triumphantly chuckled to herself as the drawer revealed its contents, but suddenly she noticed all the objects on top of the dresser wobbling precariously. Nan's old ornate mirror wobbled, the two candlesticks either side quivered, the family pictures trembled and the antique musical box shuddered. Mum paused like a cat ready to pounce on anything that dared fall to the floor, but then on the other side of the dresser she noticed something had already fallen and was in mid flight and on a crash course with the carpet below…

'MY WINE!' yelled mum, leaping up instantly to try and catch the enormous glass, which was still half full. But Mum was too late. The wine glass hurled itself towards the ground like a kamikaze pilot and bounced off the rug, relieving its contents all over the Magic Carpet.

SPLOOOOOOOSH!

'And they're off!' yelled Heron over the tannoy back at the Carpet Slipper Race. The starting gun had fired and all ten Soldier Ants had leapt into action.

Slipper racing was like race-walking but in your slippers - you weren't allowed to run, just walk as fast as you could.

The crowd roared with excitement. Finally, a proper race was underway! Each ant started from the centre of the arena and slowly spiralled out, leading them on different pathways through the thickest parts of the Magic Carpet. Then anything could happen - it was all about survival.

'Oh, what a great race, Finch,' said Heron. 'Look at ant number three go! He's way out in front, closely followed by ant number nine!' Ant number nine started to wave at the crowd at hearing his name mentioned, but suddenly tripped and fell to the ground.

OOOOOH!!! came a gasp from the audience. Ant number nine picked himself up and glared back at Heron and Finch in the commentary box.

Suddenly, from the heavens up above, the blues and whites of the afternoon change to a dull and gloomy maroon. Then spots of what felt like rain started to spatter all around the arena. People in the crowd immediately reach for their brollies and raincoats.

'Err, I'm not sure what that is, ladies and gentlemen. *HICCUP!* But it looks like we might get a spot of rain in the Magic Carpet this afternoon!' said Finch looking puzzled.

'You can't get rain indoors!' cried Heron taking a glance up at the sky.

Suddenly an enormous gust of fruity wind gushed through the arena. Grannies shivered and wriggled as the chill got in places it shouldn't. Children hugged close to their parents for warmth and the ant contenders, who were all dressed in shorts and vests, shuddered with the bitter nip in the air. Suddenly…

SSSPLAAAAAASSSSSSSSSHHHH!!!!!!!!
The entire arena turned red as gallons and gallons AND some more gallons of red wine spilled over the Magic Carpet. Everyone got completely drenched instantly. The Lord Mayor and his skinny wife, who were standing on the podium, looked like drowned rats. Their

best clobber was stained bright red and completely ruined. The ants, who were usually dark red, had turned a bright shade of Merlot and the entire audience around the arena looked like they'd taken a bath in red ink! What a sight indeed.

Heron and Finch were the only two creatures sheltered from the winey downpour, protected by their little commentary box.

Immediately, the crowd started to giggle. Then the Lord Mayor and his wife started to chuckle. The Mayor's moustache twitched as he started to lose composure and then all the contenders around the arena, including the Ant Army, started to laugh out loud in hysterics.

People were rolling about on their backs, clutching their sides in pain, sniggering, tittering, snorting and jiggling; some were hiccupping and burping, cackling and guffawing. The ants on the racetrack were wandering off all over the place: one soldier ant had started to skip in his slippers like a girl in the playground; another ant sat down and started to dribble, rocking back and forth like a baby in a pram; then another ant started to conduct a few of his chums to a sing song and another one even had the cheek to go up to the Queen of the Ants and start to chat her up! She wasn't amused at all, until she too gave into the silly hysterics that had infected the entire arena. She put her royal hand to her royal mouth and blushed and suddenly let out the most enormous girly laugh you have ever heard followed by a hiccup. She immediately hugged the brave little soldier ant and, not realising her own strength, squashed him in the process...

SPLAT!

Heron and Finch look at each other, shaking their heads.

'They're all drunk!' exclaimed Heron,

'It's disgraceful, Heron,' said Finch. 'I've never seen such mayhem. *HICCUP!*'

'Don't you start!' shouted Heron.

Suddenly the most noble of them all gave in to the drunken silliness. Lord Twitching, the royal and most honourable leader of the ants, stood in the middle of the arena and started to dance. (Very badly may I add.) He danced like your dad dances at a party. His hands were high in the air, his bum wiggled from side to side and one foot stomped up and down and out of time with the music coming from the soldier ants. His enormous soggy moustache dangled, dripping red wine as he jiggled about. He too started to sing, then on hearing this awful warbling, the crowd suddenly broke out into song. But no one knew what song was exactly being sung and all you could hear was an awful droning noise coming from the Magic Carpet.

The only one who had yet again managed to sleep through the entire commotion was the old cat Gingerbags. He was still curled up in a giant ginger fluff-ball, snoring away as usual, oblivious to the big booze-up going on around him.

Back at the Twisted Forest, after Bogey was reunited with his other missing slipper, Smell and Fluff were getting acquainted with a new friend.

'Very nice to meet you,' said Smell, putting out his hand to greet the very pretty Hiccup. She was still dressed as a cowgirl and her dreamy eyes melted Smell with one glance.

'And you too,' she said. Her smile filled Smell with happiness and made his knees wobble.

'Err, are you around for long?' enquired Fluff, putting her hand out and nudging Smell's away.

'Well, my friend and my father have been infected by the mould and they've both disappeared, so I'm trying to find them.' Hiccup looked around at the towering, twisted carpet. It looked thick and foreboding. She'd never ventured out this far from Scrag End before. She felt lonely and vulnerable without Burp and her father by her side.

'Don't worry, Hiccup,' said little Crumb. 'We're here now and we'll help you find Burp *and* your father.' He put a crumbly arm around her and smiled.

That afternoon, as the friends walked from the Twisted Forest and made their way to the main arena in time for Bogey's first Slipper Race, Bogey and Smell were way out in front and catching up on the strange things they'd seen deep in the forest.

Bogey told Smell about the two strange ghosts they'd met, the weird mould infesting the Magic Carpet and the disappearance of Burp. Smell told Bogey about the creepy figures he'd seen deep in the Twisted Forest and his visit from Dribble. He didn't mention the vision he'd had of Bogey.

'There's something afoot, Smelly, and I don't like it one bit! It's enough to put me off me dinner!' said Bogey as he walked in his reunited carpet slippers.

Crumb was still trying to chat up the lovely Hiccup and getting nowhere. Fluff was unusually quiet and dragging behind at the back of the pack. She looked down at her fingers - they'd started to tingle and itch and the usual pale-whites of her fluffy hands were changing to a mouldy grey...

Chapter Eight

Bogey's Big Race

By the time Smell and Bogey and friends arrived at the arena, everyone in the Magic Carpet was completely and utterly intoxicated!

'What in the Magic Carpet is going on here?!' yelled Smell. The entire arena was giggling and sniggering - even the Mayor and his wife had lost it...

'Oh Smeggy and Bogust! Welly wimple back to the arena. We farted you'd diddled a runner or somefink!' wibbled the Mayor, still suffering from Word Flu and now completely and utterly smashed. Mrs Mayor steadied him just in time as he wobbled from side to side.

That afternoon, Smell and Bogey and friends went around all the contenders with strong coffee in the hope of sobering them up in time for Bogey's big race. Most of the crowd had nodded off in a drunken snooze. Then, over the tannoy, came the all-important announcement.

'Ladies and Gentlemen, grubs, bugs and thingy me bobs!' announced Heron. 'Let this afternoons' games begin!!' The sound of Heron's voice reverberated around the drowsy stadium. A quiet ripple of clapping could just be heard over the enormous rumbling of snoring going on.

'Now remember all your training, Boges!' said Smell as he polished Bogey's slippers to give them extra speed. The other contenders were limbering up too. Whiff and Whatnot were preparing for their second race while dust mites Gnarl and Barkley were twitching and raring to go and two new characters had appeared on the starting block. They were fluffy creatures no one had seen before.

'Who are those two over there, Bogey?' pointed Hiccup.

'I have no idea,' said Bogey, looking a bit worried with all the stiff competition surrounding him.

'Don't worry, Boges. You've a had a year of training. You're on fire! Just you wait and see, Hiccup. There's no stopping him this year!' said Smell as he fitted Bogey's slippers to his feet.

'I'm on fire!' said Bogey unconvincingly.

The two fluffy characters looked strange. They looked down at their feet and hardly moved at all. In her usual friendly way, Fluff went over to say hello but got no response.

'I don't like the look of them two, Smell.' said little Crumb. Then suddenly, over the tannoy…

'Teams, take your places! Contenders, get ready!' bellowed Finch.

'By flibble me hiccups! And may all of those who sail in her!' yelled the Mayor. By now he'd collapsed into a drunken dribbling heap on the floor.

Smell whispered into Bogey's ear to give him one last bit of advice, then picked up his training things and made his way to the side of the track to watch the race with the others.

'Come on, Bogey! yelled Hiccup with excitement. Bogey waved over to his fan club. Suddenly Whiff, who was standing next to Bogey, started to sneeze violently…

AGHHH – TISSSUUUEEE - AGHHH – TISSSUUUEEE – SPLAT!! he sneezed as an enormous ball of snotty mucus flew out of his mouth and splattered poor old Bogey right in the ear-hole.

'EURGH!' Bogey yelled as he shook his head violently in disgust.

Just then, the starting marshal stretched out the starting ribbon and got ready to fire his starting gun in the right direction this time. He wobbled slightly, still a little hung over. The contenders crouched and waited for the gunshot...

BANG!!!!!!

They're off! ... Well everyone accept Bogey that was! All the other contenders leapt from their starting blocks and flew, leaving poor old Bogey behind still wiggling his ear. It was so blocked up with snot he hadn't heard the gunshot!

'Go Bogey go!!!' yelled Smell jumping up and down. Bogey immediately realised he was the only one left and suddenly sprung into action. When I say 'sprung', I actually mean he'd started moving like a beached green whale. By this time he was the only contender in sight - all the others had made it to the edge of the arena and were about to enter the surrounding forest.

First to disappear was Whiff. There was no stopping him! His bum wiggled from side to side, long dangly nose hair trailed behind him as he walked with speed in his super fast Zodiac Flash. Behind him was Gnarl the dust mite, who was closing on Whiff fast. The two strange fluffy creatures followed behind, their faces utterly fanatical with eyes wide open.

Suddenly, one of the white fluffy creatures jumped onto the back of Gnarl, then the other fluffy creature jumped onto Whiff! They both struggled and struggled until suddenly the struggle was over. Whiff and Gnarl stood up and stared vacantly at the two fluffy creatures. Their mouths were wide open. Their eyes blackened and their skin started to change to ashen grey. They had been ZOMBIFIED!

As each new contender entered the forest, the zombified creatures including Gnarl and Whiff pounced, and after a brief scuffle all the contenders were zombified one by one…

'Come on Boges!' yelled Hiccup and Smell. They could just about see Bogey hobbling along. He was still fiddling with his ear hole – he could hardly hear a thing and was very disorientated by the snotty blockage. By the time *he* got to the forest he was out of breath and totally lost.

'This isn't the entrance to the forest,' he thought, looking around. 'Oh flumps! Now where do I go?' he puzzled. Immediately the carpet threads did their thing again and opened up a new pathway before him.

'Oh not again,' he thought as he gingerly started to walk forward...

Meanwhile back at the start, the cheering had calmed down whilst the contenders were out of sight. No one had seen the contenders being zombified.

'How long does it take before they get back?' asked Hiccup.

'It shouldn't be that long,' replied Smell. 'They've all had extensive training and the course is well marked out.'

'Anyone for a cuppa?' shouted Mrs Mayor. Well this was greeted with several approving cries and everyone settled down to a well-earned rest and a bit of a natter.

'Hiccup!' hiccupped the Mayor, looking rather worse for wear.

Smell and Crumb started nattering to Hiccup, Barkley had started nattering to Whatnot and the two Fleas Heron and Finch, who were very chuffed that a race had finally got off the starting blocks, also joined in with the tea party. It was only after fifteen minutes or so that little Crumb, whilst munching into a rather delicious gingernut biscuit, realised that one of them was missing.

'Where's Fluff?' he yelled looking around. Immediately Smell jumped to his feet and started to scour the arena. Fluff was nowhere to be seen!

'Fluff!' he yelled at the top of his voice. But nothing…

'Fluff!!' he yelled again. Panic started creeping into his toes and worked up his legs, crippling him as he stumbled to the floor.

'She couldn't have got far, Smell,' said Crumb, trying to comfort him.

They gazed around the arena but fear was clawing its way into Smell's mind and sending shivers down his spine.

'I'm sure she's fine old chap!' said the Mayor, starting to feel a little more sober after several cups of tea. 'We'll break out a search party! We'll soon have her back safe and sound, you'll see!'

That afternoon, as the light of day faded, Smell and friends left the arena in the hunt for

Fluff. Smell was feeling the weight of the world on his shoulders.

'I shouldn't have been talking to Hiccup,' he thought to himself, feeling terribly guilty. Little Crumb offered to stay back at the Mayor's house, which overlooked the main arena to wait for Bogey's return, but the daylight had already started to fade and there was still no sign of any of the contenders. The sky became a deep dusty blue. The crickets had come out to play cricket. The bats had come out to bat and even the ghosts had come out to wicket-keep.

What had happened to Fluff? Who had set upon the other contenders and would Bogey ever make it back to the finish line and be crowned Carpet Slipper Champion?

'Oh I'm lost!' cried Bogey in a huff as he sat down to rest. He'd been going round and round for ages and got completely befuddled. The tall, woolly threads of carpet swayed above him in the early evening breeze.

'I'm totally and utterly and completely lost!!' he said again, giving up hope.
Suddenly, from the other side of the forest, something caught Bogey's eye. He squinted to try and make sense of it...

'Farty Bumflump!' he whispered under his breath. The ghostly, pale figure stared at Bogey transfixed. His face was white, his eyes were wide open and still he had nothing on his feet! The figure moved closer to Bogey, sending the willies up and down Bogey's spine. The figure didn't walk – he just hovered on the breeze glowing brightly. Bogey coward into a corner, trying to get out of the spirit's way. The figure came right up to Bogey and looked down, pointing at his slippers.

Bogey was frozen to the spot with fear. He tried to speak but what came out was...

'WWWW – BBBBBB – VVVVVV!'

The spooky figure bobbed up and down, still focused intently on Bogey's tartan slippers. Bogey had gone completely white with fright by now and was pretty close to passing out. Bogey pointed at his slippers and immediately Farty Bumflump moved closer still.

'DDDDo you www-want these?' Bogey managed to blurt out nervously.

The ghost smiled at him and placed his arms out in front. Bogey took off his Zodiac White-Stripe straight away and placed them on the floor in front of the ghoulish figure. Farty Bumflump walked forward and gently placed his feet into the comfy cosy slippers. He smiled a creepy but satisfied smile. Just then, his image flickered and faded, leaving the slippers on their own. Bogey thought he'd seen the ghost gesturing to follow him. Suddenly, the slippers started to walk away on their own!

Farty Bumflump had completely vanished but every now and then Bogey could just make out his tall lanky shape as he walked with his slippers on. He quickly started to follow them through the darkened forest.

'He must have taken my slippers in the first place,' Bogey thought to himself, remembering all those slippers he'd found underneath the kitchen floor.

Bogey had been walking for some time. The night air was chilly and all around him he could hear the yelps and screams from the creatures you wouldn't want to meet at this time of night. Just then, the most amazing sight appeared before Bogey's eyes, filling him with joy and happiness. The carpet threads opened up to reveal the main arena in the centre of the Magic Carpet. Bogey jumped and punched the air with his fists in elation and excitement. His slippers walked forward into the arena and back to the start/finish line. There was no one about. The crowds had gone home and the stands were completely empty. All that remained was the litter blowing about and the smell of red wine floating on the breeze.

'Well, that's charming isn't it!' said Bogey, miffed that nobody had stayed around to watch him finish the race. Just then, he noticed the finish line at the centre of the track...

'Um... Mr Bumflump,' he said politely, 'would you mind just crossing that line over there?' The image of Farty Bumflump suddenly appeared for a moment, his little moustache twitched and Bogey could just make out a big cheesy grin. Immediately, Bogey's slippers walked forward and with one final step crossed the finish line, completing Bogey's race. For the very first time, Bogey had completed a race! The slippers jumped into the air with glee. Bogey had finished a race! OK, the slippers weren't on Bogey's feet, but there was nothing in the rules that said you had to be in your slippers to complete a race: as long as your slippers crossed the finish line, it didn't matter who or what was wearing them.

Bogey jumped into the air and screamed with joy.

'WEEE - OOOOOO - EEEE!!!!' he yelled to himself as the lights went on in Mr Mayor's house. The curtains twitched, then a tiny little door opened and two small figures walked slowly over to where Bogey stood. The night was now black: the crickets had stopped for tea, the bats had finished batting and even the other ghosts had called it a night. Just then, Bogey noticed his slippers turning to walk away. He heard a voice in his head say, 'You'll be safe here, remember you're not alone...' Bogey smiled and held up one hand to wave...

'Thank you, Mr Bumflump... Thank you...'

Chapter Nine

Zombies

Little Crumb and the Mayor of the Magic Carpet welcomed an excited Bogey back and congratulated him on a triumphant Carpet Slipper win. Bogey couldn't believe he'd actually won - he'd never won anything before. Ever! The mayor explained that all the other contenders had mysteriously not returned and even some of the crowd had vanished too. He handed Bogey the Carpet Slipper Trophy, onto which was the carved inscription: *Farty Bumflump 1859.* Bogey smiled and looked out into the forest with pride…

The fact that no other contender had made it back to the finish line didn't dampen Bogey's spirits at all and he was quite full of himself until Crumb told him what had happened that afternoon.

'So where did Fluff go?' asked Bogey, concerned.

'We don't know, Boges. Smell and the others went to look for her but *they* didn't come back either,' said little Crumb. 'And that was hours ago!'

Bogey looked worried.

'We must go looking for them, they could be in danger!' said Bogey.

'Now don't you worry, boys!' said the Mayor. 'Everything will be fine – you'll see.' He put a comforting arm around them both and marched them back to his house for a late night cup of cocoa…

Meanwhile, deep in the Twisted Forest, a haunting mist had closed in on Smell, Hiccup, Heron, Finch and the rest of the search party…

'Fluff! FLUFF!! FLUFF!!!' shouted Smell. He twitched and jumped at every noise coming from the foreboding forest.

'Whiff! Oh Whiffy!!' shouted Whatnot.

'Gnarls! GNARLS!!' shouted Barkley.

The threads of carpet swayed in the breeze as flashes from Smell's torchlight pierced their way into the thickening woods.

'Maybe she went home, Smell?' said Hiccup. The thought of a night out deep in the Twisted Forest wasn't that appealing. She'd heard of strange things happening to people in the Twisted Forest - things that couldn't be explained...

'But why would she have left us?' replied Smell.

'Maybe she got jealous of us?' answered Hiccup.

'Jealous of us? Why would she be jealous of us?!' Smell pushed deeper into the thick overgrowth, bashing down the bushes with his torch. It was becoming harder and harder to move.

'Haven't you seen the way she looks at you, Smell? It's obvious she really likes you.'

Smell suddenly stopped in his tracks and bowed his head in sadness…

'FLUFF! WHERE ARE YOU!!!!' he screamed at the top of his voice. Heron and Finch looked over to Smell and Hiccup. Barkley and Whatnot both walked over to Smell in a show of support. There was plenty of rivalry between them all but everyone loved Fluff. Hiccup rested her hand on Smell's shoulder as the night breeze howled and whizzed past their ears, the mist had now turned into a thick icy fog that bit like sharp teeth. The Magic Carpet was uneasily quiet…

Smell had started to think all was lost and he'd never see his beloved Fluff again when something very unusual happened. All around them the thick fog began to glow intensely bright. Hiccup took a step back and shielded her eyes from the glow.

'What is it Smell?' she called out as the wind whizzed fast and tickled her ears.

'Um... *HICCUP!* Um errr *HICCUP!*' said Finch looking completely gormless.

'I don't like the look of this, Finchy me boy,' said Heron as he looked around for a handy escape route.

'Isn't this our cue to leave?' said Whatnot. 'I've heard very strange things about the Twisted Forest at night.' He tried to remove some of the bits and bobs he'd picked up along the way, to try lighten the load a little.

The fog was getting thicker - it seemed to be pulsing and growing with the light. A deep rumbling noise could just be heard above the howl of the wind. Then suddenly the carpet threads that towered all around like trees started to shake. They too seemed to be pulsing and glowing in the fog. Creaking and crackling noises started to drown out the wail of the wind as huge white hands appeared in the fog and clawed at the threads of carpet, pulling them to the ground.

Smell and the gang stumbled backward as the huge carpet threads came crashing down.

The fog was now a piercing, brilliant white. You couldn't see anything but the shear blinding light. Everything the fog came into contact with immediately turned white, crackling with its icy touch.

Smell quickly looked for a way out, but there wasn't one. All the carpet threads around them had joined together to form a perfect circle - they were now trapped. Just then, Smell noticed part of the fog had started to form into what looked like a hideous twisted face and either side of him, two claw-like hands were reaching out. He shook his head and blinked in the hope he was seeing things but as he looked again, the face became clearer and more repulsive. Smell quickly grabbed his hover-pants from his pocket and hastily put them on.

'QUICK! GRAB ONTO ME!' he yelled to his friends, but the swirling howl of the wind made it hard for Smell's voice to be heard. Hiccup immediately grabbed hold of Smell. He held her hand tight and stopped breathing - instantly they shot up several feet into the air. He was a little out of flying practice but the grubby pair of underpants leapt into action. Smell's training with Dribble soon came back to him.

'Heron! Finch! Grab on!!' he yelled down as the pair of fleas ran around like headless chickens. Heron and Finch both grabbed onto

Hiccup and immediately they too are pulled up and away from danger.

The face in the fog intensified, letting out an almighty roar. The wind buffeted Smell and the rest as they dangled for dear life. Smell's ears suddenly went pop with the pressure of the wind.

'Whatnot! Barkley! Up here!!' yelled Heron, looking down at the remaining two.

Whatnot and Barkley jumped and managed to grab hold of one of Finch's long, dangly legs. They very slowly rose off the ground, putting a strain on the tower of floating people. Just then Smell let out a gasp of air! He'd ran out of breath... He quickly breathed in again and the dangly tower of friends jolted toward the ground.

'Higher! Get higher!!' yelled Heron in a panic. He could see the foggy white claws of the beast below and they were only inches away from Barkley's feet. By now the creature had fully formed: its eyes were black like coals, its fingernails were sharp and pointy, its mouth a bottomless chasm and its nose needed a right good blowing!

'Oooh help!' screamed the little dust mite as he turned to see the foggy white talons of the creature miss his foot by a claw.

Smell tried to flap his hands to get higher but it was no good - the weight of everyone was too great. They just hovered in mid air whilst Smell's face turned bluer and bluer.

The beast below roared again. The intense light got brighter as its claws reached out for Barkley.

'Arrrggghhh! It's got me! It's got me!' he screamed in fear.

The foggy beast grabbed Barkley's leg and tugged at the tower of floating friends. Two sharp pointy fangs appeared in the fog and engulfed Barkley. He screamed and then… he was gone.

'Smell, go higher! You've got to get higher!' yelled Hiccup. *'It's got Barkley!'*

Smell was now completely blue all over and becoming light headed with the lack of air. He took another gasp and for an instant the tower of friends jolted up and away from the foggy menace below, revealing the remains of Barkley dangling below. He was still holding onto Finch's leg but was now completely and utterly ashen-grey. His eyes were a piercing brilliant white and his mouth was wide open. He'd been ZOMBIFIED!

'AARRRGGGHHH!!!' screamed Hiccup.

'Oohhh, Smell! Go higher. Please!' yelled Whatnot. The fear and dread in his eyes made Hiccup shiver with fright. Suddenly the zombified remains of Barkley sprung into action. He looked up at Whatnot with a vacant, soulless stare. Whatnot yelped in fright as the fog enveloped him!

'ARRGGGHHH! It's got Whatnot too!!!' yelled Hiccup, petrified.

'I… can't… hold it!' cried Smell. The tower wobbled again and started to fall to the ground as Smell ran out of breath. The pulsing hideous beast below growled with delight. Its evil eyes glowed brighter and its talons opened ready to devour its prey. Just then, Heron lost his grip and Hiccup's foot flew out of his hand, hurling him, Finch and the two-zombified remains of Barkley and Whatnot to the ground.

'ARRRRGGGGHHHH!!!!!' Heron and Finch both yelled as they fell. Smell and Hiccup bolted upward immediately, sending them far above the foggy beast. The malevolent creature roared in anger.

Heron and Finch had landed on a soft pile of twisted carpet. They immediately crouched their bodies down low, channelled all their energy into their legs and sprung high into the air. Fleas were very cunning and amazing jumpers; they could jump for miles if they wanted.

The beast ignored the two Fleas and concentrated back on Smell and Hiccup.

'We are flying, Smell! We can fly!' cried Hiccup. With the weight of the others gone Smell could now manoeuvre his underpants.

'Right, let's get out of here!' he cried, looking for a clear path in the foggy haze. They could see for miles across the Magic Carpet. Twinkling specks of light from people's homes glistened like dying embers in a fire. Smell could just make out the flagpole in the main arena stretching high into the night sky. He thought of Bogey and the others and wondered if they were alright.

The beast below suddenly calmed. Its glowing light dimmed and its roar turned to a murmur…

'Smelly... Smelly hear us...' came a faint voice from below. Smell's ear pricked up and fidgeted, thinking they'd heard a familiar sound.

'Smelly, hear us! ...Hear me!!'

Smell stopped instantly and stared back down at the ground.

'What are you waiting for, Smell? Let's go!' said Hiccup, clinging on to Smell tightly...

'Smelly, hear me. Don't leave me, please!' came the voice again. It was soft and fearful. Smell immediately let out his breath and glided back to Earth.

'What are you doing, Smell? The beast below... look out!' cried Hiccup.
Smell didn't say a word as clumps of fog swirled calmly around them as they descended.

'Come to me, Smelly. Don't leave me here. Please save me... Smelly, hear us...'

Smell and Hiccup drifted through the cold, misty air, edging nearer and nearer to the beast, but it seemed to be dissolving in the wind. All that remained were its claws twitching powerlessly in the breeze.

Smell and Hiccup glided toward the Magic Carpet, parting the fog as they fell. Just then Smell saw a sight that lifted his heart and filled him with such emotion. Below their feet appeared the familiar sight of Fluff reaching out with both hands.

'Smelly, I'm here. Come save me!' cried a terrified Fluff. She was unusually pale and her eyes were blackened as she stood in the middle of the swirling mist.

'It's Fluff! Look, it's Fluff!' screamed Smell in excitement. He quickly sped up their descent. Hiccup stared closely at the fluffy meek figure standing below. The fog swirled around her. Hiccup felt uneasy.

'Fluff! Are you all right?' said Smell as his toes finally touched down. Fluff suddenly ran to embrace him and flung her arms around him. Her touch fizzed and tingled against his skin. Smell was so pleased to see her. He thought she was gone forever and now he was holding her tight.

'I will never let you go again, Fluff! Never! I promise!'

Hiccup noticed movement from all around them. The white zombies were watching them from inside the foggy cloud. Some hid behind threads of carpet. Their glowing eyes were dulled but their stare was firm.

'Smell, let's get out of here. It's not safe, look!' She pointed to the creatures.

Smell tried to turn and look but he couldn't. He couldn't move an inch! Suddenly the tingle of Fluff's touch intensified. It felt more like a sting as every part of his body electrified.

'Fluff, you're hurting me. Stop it!' he screamed, trying to break free.

'Smell! What's happening?' cried Hiccup, standing back in horror.

Smell struggled to break free from Fluff's grip but she was too strong. Her fluffy fibres had connected to him. Slowly, they wrapped their way around his arms and feet. The sting suddenly increased and rushed up his spine and into his head. He struggled again, trying to push Fluff away, but he could not get free.

'Fluff! Stop it!! Please sto…'

Suddenly Smell went silent. Hiccup backed away, edging nearer and nearer to the zombies that hid in the fog. They just stared at Smell, fixated…

'NO!!!!' screamed Hiccup as she turned to run. The zombies suddenly sprung into action, grabbing hold of her arm. Their touch tingled and itched as she too struggled to get free. Grappling with the soulless creatures, Hiccup watched Smell change from his usual transparent self into a grey, characterless ghost. Fluff was still holding onto him tight. Her body began to glow and her fluffy hairs jolted and whizzed with energy.

Smell had been absorbed!

Fluff and Smell became one glowing entity as the white fibres grew and grew over their bodies until Hiccup could not recognise them anymore. Just a white ball of energy glowed bright as the surrounding mist drew closer in the gloomy forest. Then to her horror, the remaining zombies turned their attention to her…

Hiccup slowly moved away, looking for an escape route, but it was no use. She was trapped. One of the zombies walked forward with its arms out in front and with eyes like empty caves, the creature smiled…

Hiccup froze to the spot in fear. No, not fear - it was shock. She stared at the ghostly figure before her, then dread filled her sweet little body as she realised what she was looking at. Or rather who she was looking at. Tears began to fill her eyes… *'Daddy ?'* she whispered…

Chapter Ten

The Hairy Blob

'There's somebody watching us!' said Finch, looking spooked as he walked.

'Will you relax, Finch? It's the middle of the night, we're lost deep in the Twisted Forest, we're miles from anywhere and you *think* we're being watched? Of course we are! There's probably all sorts of weirdo creepy creatures looking at you right now!' said Heron. He was trying to concentrate on finding a way out of the Twisted Forest. The friendly Fleas wandered aimlessly as the early morning dawn chorus began to spring into full song…

'What was that? yelped Finch. His ears pricked toward the sky.

'It's a Grub,' said Heron, striding ahead with a false sense of direction. An enormous shrilling, chilling and thrilling sound echoed around the Magic Carpet. It sounded like something really, *really* horrible, smelly and revolting with a really bad cough.

'A Grub? What's a grub?' said Finch, puzzled.

'It's a thing with no eyes, no ears, no nose, no nothing!' replied Heron.

'Oh! …No nose, how does it smell?'

'Horrible!' said Heron, as he chuckled to himself. He suddenly stopped dead in his tracks and stared at the blackened forest in front of him.

'Boys! Help me…' came a gruff and familiar voice. Heron and Finch froze to the spot and looked at each other in fright. The hairs on their legs stood to attention like prickly thorns. Heron could just make out a small creature bent over and moving in the dark, but before he could investigate further he noticed something else. The mould clawing at the carpet threads had started to grow! White hairs were emerging from the snowy fungus and growing at an alarming rate.

'Quick, Finch. Scarper!' shouted Heron and without another thought Heron and Finch crouched down, clicked their legs into gear and…

WHISSSSHHH!!!!! They disappeared in a blink of the eye.

The Mayor and his lady wife had served up a third round of cocoa by this time. Bogey and Crumb slouched on the comfy sofa, clutching at their bellies. The quaint little cottage overlooked the main arena and for a brief moment felt like a safe haven.

'I must say, Mrs Mayor, you really know how to make the most delicious biscuits,' munched Crumb, now on his third.

'Why thank you! They're chocolate chip cookies actually.'

Crumb looked down at the crumbs on his lap in horror. *After all, he was a chocolate chip cookie!* He quickly brushed them off in a panic. Bogey wanted to giggle but giggling was the last thing he felt like doing right now. His thoughts were with Smell and Fluff. What had happened to them and *what* was happening to the Magic Carpet?

Through the gap in the curtain, Mr Mayor could see swarms of carpet dwellers marching into the twisted forest. They were pale like ghosts, glowing in the frosty morning light. Blank, lifeless faces passed the mayor's house one by one. Fidget the mumbler, Mrs Hair the next door neighbour carrying her toaster, Whiff and Gnarl, Fangs the spider and even the local tramp Bob the Slob all walked into the forest transfixed and zombified.

'Are they all leaving?' said Bogey, looking concerned.

'They all seem brainwashed. Whatever's gotten into them?' replied the Mayor. He shook his head and mopped his brow with an old, snotty hanky.

'Maybe Gingerbags can help?' said Crumb. His voice trembled.

'If *he* hasn't gone the same way…' Bogey replied.

Life in the Magic Carpet was being wiped out one by one. Everywhere had become baron: no movement, no noise, no nothing.

'Ooh, I say. Look!' exclaimed Mr Mayor. Through the gap in the curtains, he caught a glimpse of something and it wasn't pale and white - it was rich in colour.

'What is it?' worried Crumb.

Bogey too peered through the gap in the curtains. 'Quick, open the door!' he yelled. 'It's Heron and Finch! Quick, open the door!' He immediately grabbed hold of the door handle and ran out to greet them without thinking. He'd never been so happy to see a couple of fleas.

'Heron! Finch! Are you OK?'

'Yes, just... we've had to dodge some dodgy looking characters on the way!' said Heron.

'Where are Smell and Fluff and the others?'

'They're gone,' said Finch. 'The carpet is being absorbed and everyone with it... *HICCUP!*'

'Gone? How?' said Crumb, peering from the Mayor's front door.

Heron and Finch explained what had happened to Smell and friends. Bogey, Crumb and Mr and Mrs Mayor just listened, bemused. They felt helpless and trapped in their little puny cottage.

'You didn't see any other life out there?' asked Crumb. He was starting to feel quite spooked; memories of his old home in Scrag End came rushing back to him.

'Well, the only life we saw was pretty lifeless life,' replied Finch.

'Come in and close that door quickly!' said Mrs Mayor.

Outside, the morning light dimmed suddenly. A crunching sound vibrated the walls of the cottage as they buckled from the strain of the strangling tentacles that now surrounded it.

'Oooh! It's the end!' cried Mrs Mayor. She cowered in the corner, clutching her handbag.

An unearthly, foreboding and intense white glow pierced through the gap in the curtains. Mouldy tentacles stretched over the roof and clawed their way round to the back of the house. Crumb and Mr and Mrs Mayor huddled together for comfort, blinded by the light. Heron and Finch had slipped into the cupboard under the stairs for protection - if there was one place that would surely be safe, it was under the stairs. Bogey moved toward the front door and rested his hand on the door handle. Through the door-window he could see the desolation and mouldiness outside and it was now everywhere. The arena was unrecognisable! White, scrawny tentacles grew out from the ground and curled their way into the air like weeds. The Magic Carpet and the people were all being absorbed... but by what?

The once magical rug had become a desolate, unmagical place. The sound of zombified feet could be heard marching for miles around. The Mayor's little cottage slowly succumbed to the towering tentacles that strangled the life out of everything it touched.

Inside the cottage, Bogey paced up and down in the Mayor's favourite slippers. He looked tormented and confused. Crumb, the Mayor and the rest of the gang just sat at the dining table, staring at an almost empty plate of chocolate biscuits, their heads bent in defeat. No one said a word.

Bogey suddenly stopped pacing and stared through the gap in the curtains. His ears twitched to attention. The white, mouldy tentacles stretched their way over the glass like creeping ivy. Bogey turned to his remaining friends and smiled a warm smile. Crumb looked up, unsure of what Bogey was thinking. He picked up the once full plate of chocolate biscuits and pointed the last lonely biscuit at Bogey in the hope he'd sit down and eat. Bogey walked up to the plate and picked up the solitary chocolate biscuit. He suddenly remembered a happy memory: the thought of his chocolate chip cookies sprouting arms and legs and running for dear life. The memory seemed such a long time ago.

As he munched on the last chocolate biscuit, he looked at Crumb with affection.

'Thank you, my friend…'

Bogey turned around and paused for a moment… He took a very deep breath and then with confidence, he walked straight toward the front door, grabbed hold of the brass door handle and before anyone had the chance to react, he'd opened the door and walked straight out into the blinding white light outside.

'NO, BOGEY!!' screamed Crumb. But it was too late. The mouldy tentacles immediately swallowed him up. Crumb watched on as the vivid greens of Bogey's skin turned to ashen grey and then… he was gone!

Outside, the giant, mouldy creature had become monstrous. A huge, devouring blob grew in the centre of the Magic Carpet, pulsing with energy and power. Everywhere glowed white, the tentacles had clawed their way into the ground like tree roots from which fine, white hairs spread to every corner of the carpet. Just a baron, unmagical wasteland remained. Little Crumb was now left on his own. His friends were all gone and his home was now unrecognisable.

Deep in the once magical carpet, at the place known as Dribble's Leap, a few patches of carpet were untouched by the mouldy invader. The pit was a place for shelter and staring up from the darkness, one blood-red eye watched and waited, silently…

***Smell & Bogey* will return in… '*Smell & Bogey and the Giant Hairy Blob!*'**